VIA Folios 134

Not for Nothing

Not for Nothing

GLIMPSES INTO A JERSEY GIRLHOOD

Kathy Curto

BORDIGHERA PRESS

Library of Congress Control Number: 2018910243

Some names in this book have been changed. The events and experiences offered here are glimpses of time, reimagined.

Printed in the United States.

Published by
BORDIGHERA PRESS
John D. Calandra Italian American Institute
25 West 43rd Street, 17th Floor
New York, NY 10036

VIA FOLIOS 134
ISBN 978-1-59954-129-7

CONTENTS

III. One More Thing about Now

For my dream team, Peppe, AJ, Maya, Maisy and Sam

If light is in your heart, you will find your way home.

—RUMI

I. NOW

When I was growing up in southern New Jersey in the 1970s and 80s there were days my mother floated through the halls of our brick ranch house leaving behind waves and wafts of curious and enticing aromas: Charlie, Wind Song and, if she'd been cooking all day, garlic.

"So what's the story, Morning Glory?" she'd ask.

Then, a kiss on the forehead, steeped in pure comfort and warmth, her caramel skin and pink lipstick creating a glint of unfamiliar brightness.

Magic.

Then there were the other days that reeked with ambivalence and confusion. She'd toss that same question out, "What's the story, Morning Glory?" and it would land like a featherbrick on my face, prompting only silence.

I wanted to answer. Nothing came out.

I am the youngest of four and born almost ten years after my brother, so a good portion of my early years were spent feeling left out with "puss" on my face.

"Wipe that puss off your face, would you!" I'd often hear. "And smile for Chrissakes."

These days, a mother of four myself, I have a hunch the puss had to do with the fallout of what I thought was my daily predicament: I was the last to know everything yet I somehow made it my job to clean the everything up.

But having an unlocatable voice meant I excelled at eavesdropping and wondering. It also meant being on the receiving end of seemingly endless rhetorical questions.

Happy now?

Satisfied?

Are you finished?

In my house, though, the questions were asked but answers, forbidden. I learned the art of keeping my trap shut. These inquiries usually came after something got dropped on the floor, like the small heart-shaped platter filled with nuts and *finuke* my mother put out "to pick on" after a meal. Or sometimes they came after a spill, like the glass of Tab "you just had to fill to the top, didn't you?"

And there was one more question posed to me, over and over again, mostly by my big-hearted, bull-headed, *capa tosta* of a father. It typically flew my way when the cyclone of rage and love and fear and affection ripped through the walls, shaking the everyday worlds of three places: our home, the family gas station business and my girlwoman consciousness.

Who do you think you are?

* * *

This collection of flash pieces—glimpses, really—are stories built around encounters and artifacts of my Italian American, South Jersey childhood. My mother's handkerchiefs, my father's hairpieces, peppers frying on the stove, the haunting needle marks on skinny, teenage boy arms. The ocean. And the tall red head who never paid a cent for gas and had a curious way of doing two things at once, looking at my father and cracking her gum. It is a peek into the blue-collar, lipstick-on-your-collar and button-up-your-collar-and-be-a-good-girl time of life that produced as many hilarious as tragic understandings (and misunderstandings) of the world.

Happy now? Satisfied? Are you finished? What's the story? Who do you think you are?

So this book is, I suppose, the answer to some of these questions.

II. THEN

MARY JANES

Coca Cola is one of the reasons we're heading to the station, my mother and me. We got an early start this morning and we've been out making our stops. The A&P. Garden State Bank. The shoemaker and Sal the Butcher.

"Hot as hell," she says when we walk out of the bank. Then she says we should run back into the A&P and pick up some Coca Cola for my father, my brother and for all the customers at the gas station.

The A&P has two places to find soda. The warm soda is on a regular shelf in a regular aisle and cold bottles of soda are in a tall, see-through cooler in the front of the store by the registers. Whenever we are waiting to check out at A&P I stare into the clear doors and try to pick my favorite kind. Usually I end up with root beer, but sometimes cream.

So, we buy cold bottles of Coke because it's hot as hell and she thinks soda will help.

My mother is always bringing things to people.

My father introduces me to them, his customers. Customers of Fred's Texaco. We sometimes just call it the station.

"Hey, Jiggy," my father calls out to one of the regulars. "Have you met the baby of the family? This is my baby, Jig." He points to me with his cigarette.

"She don't look like no baby to me, Freddy." Jiggy's cigar hangs from his lips. "She's a pretty one. A little young lady, she is!"

Even though two of Jiggy's fingernails are yellowbrown and he has snot under his nose, I still like the way it sounds to be called pretty. I remember the first time I saw Jiggy and his fingernails. It was a few months ago and again we were there at the station. He was waiting for my father to put new tires on his car. After he shook my hand and we got back into our car I asked my mother why his nails look like that.

"Cigar," she said.

* * *

"Raindrops Keep Falling on My Head" plays on the radio that hangs from a hook next to the key to the station bathroom. This song sounds like one that's sung by a guy who wears flip flops and blue jeans.

There's a room at the station and everybody calls it the Waiting Room. That's where I am now. But I'm not waiting for anyone or anything right now, which is strange because I'm always waiting.

This song makes me happy. It makes me want to dance and sing. So, I do.

I'm up on the gold and green speckled counter, where the black adding machine is and where everybody signs the work orders and pays the bills. It's a funny thing, dancing in a spot people use for what my mother and father call the paperwork, the business.

It's the summer before my fifth birthday. Hot air sticks on me but today it's not heavy which is also strange. Today's different. I'm Shirley Temple except that my hair is black and it's very short. Jim at Joel Richard Beauty Parlor is the guy who does my mother's hair and he calls me and my haircut a pixie.

What's that mean? Pixie.

If Jim calls me a pixie because being a pixie is a good thing then today I'm a dancing pixie princess with people cheering and smiling and begging for more. They shake their heads. They holler "*Bravo! Bravo!*" They blow kisses at me and say to each other, "Where did Freddy's little girl learn to dance and sing like this? Isn't she a doll, this little one?"

I love days like this one, like today, when my father is smiling what looks like a real smile. Days like this when he lifts me so high that my feet land on top of the green and gold specks and all I feel is right, okay and good. Not worried. Not afraid. Everything is pixie pretty on days like this.

On the way up, into the air, I smell him and his uniform. Dark grey Dickies and heavy work boots. I smell him. Gasoline. Canoe. Grease. He is all those smells mixed together plus the smell of the thick green oil that Mac and my father pour into car engines. It's the oil in the lines on the sides of his fingers.

Jiggy winks and cheers and hollers and then goes back to sipping his Coke. I finish my dance. My father puts his arms out to catch me so I jump and then slide down the front of his uniform.

Gasoline. Canoe. Grease.

Oil.

My Mary Janes touch the floor and I take a bow.

"*Madonna Mia* it's hot as hell outside! Here, have something cold to drink," my mother says to the others in the room who cool themselves off and fan Reader's Digests in front of their faces. Then she hands me more bottles, one at a time, and I pass them out to everybody who's at Fred's Texaco to get their cars fixed. But I don't just walk from one customer to another.

I skip. I sing. I slide.

"Sweets, careful now," she says. "That's all we need! Soda all over the floor, for God's sake!"

But she's smiling when she says it and I'm smiling, too. I'm the best dancing pixie princess there is and, for now, things are right, okay and good.

More smiles.

More. More. More.

Now they both stand against the wall behind the counter and watch me. It's the wall where my father hangs what my mother calls the filthy, dirty clipboards. She's right. They are stained with all kinds of stuff but they're important because work orders get clipped onto them and those work orders tell everybody what people want fixed on their cars.

I keep tapping like crazy and I sing and try to wink to the customers like Shirley Temple. I twirl my yellow sundress. I do all this but still see them, standing against the wall.

My mother takes a handkerchief from her pocketbook and wipes sweat from the top of his shiny head and then his forehead full of big, thick wrinkles. Then he takes his arm and puts it around her waist and pulls her in a little. Like he wants her to be closer to him and he wants to hold on. I can't stop looking at them and especially at his hands.

That's what I see today, with the air sticking to my skin and "Raindrops" playing on the radio.

The little pink roses on her handkerchief.

The sweat on his forehead and how it drips down past his ears but sometimes gets caught in the grey hairs on the side of his face. And then it just stays there.

The way the customers' shoulders jump up a little, like when people get scared, when the bell goes off to let my father and brother know that someone is waiting to get gas.

I see all these things even when I twirl, tap, sing, wink, smile and give out Cokes to people with broken cars. But most of all I see the way my father pulls my mother in and how she stays right next to him and holds on, like it's the easiest thing in the world to do.

TRADING HAIRPIECES FOR OIL CHANGES

It's not long after my crazy love for Shirley Temple and "Raindrops Keep Falling on my Head" that my father gets his new head of hair. Silver and black. Distinguished and sharp, are the words my mother uses the first time she sees him with it on his head.

Do other fathers have shiny heads one day and hair the next? And then have to take it off every night and put it on a special holder?

My father's hairpiece holder costs a lot of money, according to my mother. It looks like a big, velvet head with no eyes and just little round marks where a nose and ears should be. Every time I have to bring something into his bathroom—like a roll of toilet paper or a box of Q-tips—I touch it. The special and very expensive velvet holder is smooth and fuzzy. It's not those cheap Styrofoam kinds, like in the dusty, smelly back room at Leo's Barber Shop. I saw two of those the last time we went to Leo's and it even looked like someone tried to draw eyes onto the white-as-snow faces with a pencil. I got goose bumps from that.

"They're not cheap, Freddy, these hairpiece holders," Leo says, "but they're classier than the rest and better for the piece!" Leo is my father's barber and he says there's nothing worse than when a customer takes his hairpiece off at night, puts it on the holder and sees it slide right off the slippery Styrofoam.

"Nothing for the piece to cling to, Freddy!" Leo says.

Leo is tall and skinny and when he tells my father about the classy holders he swings his arms in the air. Like flying seagulls, those arms of his.

Every night my father presses his eyes closed real tight and yanks the stiff, shiny new hair off of his head. He lets out a big ahhh once it's off. My mother makes the same sound when she takes her stockings off at the end of the day before she puts her apron on to get dinner started. Some nights around here when there are no messes and nobody is worrying all night long about one thing or another and my brother is following orders at the station and everybody is doing what they're supposed to be doing, my father might walk in the front door home from work—more gasoline, more broken cars—and then I follow him into his bathroom. I sit on top of the toilet seat and watch him rip the hair off of his head. I press my eyes shut. I get a chill up my back and down my arms. When I do open my eyes, I see three lines of pink blisters on his scalp and smell the stinky glue and tape he uses to stick his hair on every day. The whole thing makes my stomach do somersaults but I can't help watching.

I just can't help it.

Lisa Antonelli is a girl who lives down the street. Those blisters on my father's head remind me of the way Lisa's baby brother's rear end looked when I saw her mom change his diaper. It was red and bubbly and even though it looked a little like my father's head I didn't say any-thing. I wondered about Lisa Antonelli's father and if he ever had new hair, pink blisters and a classy holder, too.

When the hairpieces get old and the fake hair starts to look like hay, my father calls Leo and orders a new one. For two reasons, I love when this happens. First, it means I get to keep the old one to play with. I trim it and wash it, tie rubber bands on it and try to practice my braids and ponytails. And the other thing that happens when a hairpiece gets old is this: Leo comes to our house! He comes to 847 Regency Court and my father gets to sit on a stool in the middle of the kitchen under the ceiling light. My mother puts a clean dishtowel, she calls it a *moppina*, on his shoulders. Leo trims the fluffy hairs around his ears and holds little patches of fake hair next to my father's head match the color which is pretty hard because it's grey, black and white all at the same time. The whole thing is very exciting and different from any other night in our house and that's why I love when Leo comes over.

"Leo, where does that hair come from anyway?" I ask and dip the veal into the bowl with the slimy raw eggs, then into the breadcrumbs, like my mother tells me to do.

We make chicken cutlets for dinner all the time but she always makes veal for Leo when he comes to the house. "It's only right," she says, and my father nods his head up and down and tells her not to forget to make the escarole salad with the crushed red pepper because Leo likes that.

Oil changes are free for Leo because of the hairpieces and two weeks ago when Leo took his old Pinto to the shop for an oil change he kept talking about what a good cook my mother was. I bet my father liked that. Liked that Leo was bragging about her cooking. It probably made him feel like a big shot and he probably loved it when Leo said, in front of all the customers in the Waiting Room that day, "Freddy, I'm telling ya. That wife of yours, she could make meatballs outta cardboard!"

But right now, it's cutlets, not meatballs. I'm on a stool in front of the stove and next to my mother who turns them with one hand and keeps one hand in front of me. I figure that Leo doesn't hear me over the cracking oil sounds the veal makes so I ask again, "Leo, where'd you get the hair?"

Leo is the only grown-up I don't call Mister. I don't even know his last name, it's always just Leo and I guess that's ok with everybody because no one yells at me when I say things like, "Hi, Leo!" or ask him questions about where he gets the hair.

Finally, he answers. "From people who have too much, little lady," he says and winks at me.

"So, they just give it to you? Do they cut it off themselves?" I have more questions, too, like: Do they put it in a bag? Do they wash it first? But I don't ask. I don't want to act like a smart aleck.

"Don't ask so many questions, Doll," my father says, "and go get Daddy his cigarettes."

SOPHIA LOREN'S EYES

"Freddy, that's enough now," my mother screams. I don't know what's shaking more, her voice or her hands. "Drop it, now, for God's sake. Just drop it."

"No, you goddamned tramp," my father slams back. "Get the fuck out of this house and take them all with you! You're all alike. Nobody listens when I talk."

I'm sitting in the front hallway in a corner next to the coat closet that we never keep coats in. I can't see my mother's face from here but I know what it looks like. She's not crying because she never cries in the middle of the messes. Only after.

Now there's stomping and moving from one side of the kitchen to the other. I think a chair gets shoved but I can't say for sure. It could be the table.

He keeps going. "Yous don't give a shit about me. I bust my ass for you and get nothing back. Go! Get the fuck out of my house."

The round piece of metal that keeps the closet door from falling off is jabbing into me. It hurts but I don't move. I can't. I think about finding the guts and running out, maybe to the beach. The boardwalk. Maybe the bay. But even if I did find them I know I wouldn't use them because that would mean leaving her with him. There aren't enough guts for that.

I hear glass break. The back-porch door slams shut. Windows, too. This is what happens. He breaks stuff and she shuts doors and windows. Once I asked her: "How come there are always so many big fights around here?"

"Look, no one knows what goes on in other people's houses. Behind closed doors." She shook her head and made a clicking noise with her mouth that meant she was disappointed in me. Asking that question meant I wasn't thankful for what we had. After she shook and clicked for what felt like an hour she said, "Remember that."

Still it made no sense to me and I even tried a few weeks back to tell her that it didn't really work. The closing everything so tight.

"Ma, if Mr. Benton can smell your macaroni and gravy, I bet he can hear the fighting."

The Bentons have a big screened-in porch, a dog named Mootsie, a vegetable garden and coffee cans on their kitchen counter where they throw their dinner leftovers. I think it's kind of weird but Mary, the oldest in the family and my best friend, says it all gets put back into the garden.

"Oh, cool," I said when she told me that but what I really thought was Yuck, that's gross. I know Mary's dad goes crazy over my mom's cooking because he told me once that the smell makes his mouth water even when he's cutting the grass or picking out weeds on the other side of their yard. "Your mother's a queen in that kitchen!" he says over and over when I go to Mary's to play.

When I told my mom about Mr. Benton smelling her macaroni she smiled and winked. Her eyes sparkled that day, which makes sense. It was around the time she told us that from then on out she'd be doing her eyes like Sophia Loren.

I still can't see her face now but I'm pretty sure her eyes aren't sparkling. My knees are wet because I'm crying all over them, still here in this corner of the front hallway. And they hurt too, because tears sting the cuts on my knees. I was riding too fast on my bike and went flying the day before yesterday.

I keep pulling my legs closer to my chest and hold my hands around the front of my ankles. I press my head down and cover my ears.

Barry, my sister Ria's boyfriend, comes over to me. He kneels down on the floor and wipes my face with the corner of his sleeve. I didn't even know Barry was here. My sister probably called him from her bedroom and told him to come over. She probably told him she was scared and that maybe something bad might happen here. My mother says Ria has a bad habit of telling everyone her business and that she needs to toughen up. "Why do you got to tell everybody and their brother?" she's constantly asking her. I'm pretty sure that same speech included the bit about closed doors too.

I love Barry for a lot of reasons but mostly because he's nothing like anyone here and he reminds me of those people you see on TV shows who say "Peace, man." all the time. He has curly blond hair that gets very frizzy when it's hot outside. Sometimes he puts it in a ponytail which makes me laugh. He wears jeans with patches on the knees and sandals with no backs. He smells like the beach. Barry has a little yellow car with dents on both sides. There's always a Frisbee in his back seat.

Sometimes when Ria and Barry go out driving in Seaside or to Island Heights they take me with them. I love this for lots of reasons but especially because it means I get to watch Ria put her makeup on before we run to Barry's car before we hear his car. Ria's makeup is special and when she is all done putting it on she sparkles. Beautiful sister princess. Once, a couple of weeks ago we were driving back from the boardwalk and he turned the music up real loud.

"Who's singing this song?" I asked because it sounded slow and fast at the same time and the singer's voice was kind of sad. I had to keep pulling hair out of the corners of my mouth because of the wind.

"Bread," Barry said and moved one of his hands from the steering wheel to my sister's leg.

I leaned into the front seat to turn up the volume. "Bread?" I laughed and then Ria did, too. "What kind of kooky name is that?"

But now Barry's still here in the hall with me, wiping the tears from my knees with a Howard Johnson napkin he finds in his pocket. I think he calls out for my sister and then he leans closer to me and says something like, "C'mon pumpkin. All families fight. Sometimes dads lose their cool."

I look at what a mess Barry's hair is now. No ponytail, blond frizz standing up in all different places. Ria comes toward us from the kitchen doorway and she's crying hard.

Everyone's a mess.

Everything's a mess.

I hear my father bang his fist into the wall. "Yous are all alike!"

I can't see my mother from this corner by the closet but I hear the water running in the sink and then a cabinet slams.

I wonder if her eyes still look like Sophia Loren.

CALLING ME MAMA

We are sitting in Friendly's and my mother is scribbling on a form. Name, address, phone number. Stuff like that. She had asked the man at the counter for the paper even before we sat down and then he asked her if she needed a pen and if I wanted anything to eat while she was writing.

"Hey, Bumblebee," he said, "how about a vanilla milkshake while your mom fills out this application?" Nobody ever called me a bumblebee before. It's just plain stupid but the milkshake sounded good so I said, "Ma, is it ok?" and when she said "yes" we sat at the counter in these cool spinning chairs. I had never before been in a chair that made me dizzy. It was like having the Tilt-A-Whirl in a Friendly's.

So now I know that applications and forms are the same thing. We've been filling out lots of forms these days, ever since we left the house on Regency Court. I don't mind, though. Sometimes it looks like my mom minds because she gets that look on her face like she's the most tired person you've ever seen and then she starts sighing real loud as if she's letting out all the air that's left inside of her.

After she finishes writing everything down on the paper and gives it back to the guy who called me bumblebee she tells me I will start school in a few days. I stop slurping my milkshake. "Kindergarten. In a church school down the street," she says.

"It's only half-day," she whisper-talks. "You'll meet other kids, too. Even ones from here."

Here is The Princess James Apartments. We live here now because the messes got bigger and were there all the time. My mother and father had a huge fight and she said, "That's it. Enough now!" Then she called him a son of a bitch bastard and a no-good liar and he told her to get the hell out, to take us with her and that she was never woman enough for him. That part is just plain stupid, too. Of course, my mother's a woman and she's not ugly or fat and she doesn't talk weird and have greasy hair like some other mothers I see around. She's got smooth tan skin and pretty lips. She wears light pink lipstick almost every day and rubs important stuff into her skin at night before she goes to bed.

I know that part made her mad, too, because it was right after he said the *not being a woman part* that she started giving out orders. She told my oldest sister, Lucy, to get her stuff together, to figure out where Ria was and help Jack to find the keys to the Lincoln. Lucy always gets the most orders of us all.

Then she looked at me. "Put some panties in a bag. We need get the hell out of here."

"Enough now!" she kept saying over and over and over. No tears just her shaky voice and her shaky fingers. How come she's not crying? I can't believe she's not crying.

Less shaky and louder: "How dare you? You bastard!"

Then my father took the little wooden mug tree and threw it against the wall. Not only did the mugs break into a million pieces but the wooden fork and knife set that we bought on sale at K-mart and hung up the week before crashed to the ground.

I have this Captain Kangaroo suitcase I would've brought if everything was not so loud and scary and everyone was not rushing around so much, bumping and crashing into things, walls and tables and even lamps. I love Captain Kangaroo. My mother says Jack used to like him, too, but he says he never did. Sometimes he just tries to act like such a big shot. My mother tells him he better watch himself. Who cares if you like Captain Kangaroo? Now he thinks he's so cool because he gets to watch *The Flip Wilson Show* and stay out late.

"I don't need to go to school! I don't need to meet other kids!" My face burns and the sides of my head beat from underneath. Who needs other kids? We have each other. Who needs kids when there's so much stuff going on? All these forms. All these papers.

"I don't want to go to Kindergarten. I want to stay with you." Tears almost slide through. I push them back inside.

Swallow and blink. Swallow and blink.

"Listen to me, Mama," she says. My mother sometimes calls me *Mama* when she's trying to tell me something I don't want to hear or when I am sad, scared, unhappy. I don't really understand why she does this. It's weird and doesn't make any sense to me but it makes me feel better sometimes, like we'll always be together. No matter how many messes there are. And *Mama* sounds better than other dumb names grown-ups use sometimes. Like Bumblebee.

"This is what you need to do and that's that! I'm not going anywhere, for God's sake!" she says. "I'll put you on the bus and be there when the bus drops you off."

I'm trying to listen but I can't because I'm swallowing and blinking more than ever now. I can't even look at her face. I'll have to say goodbye to her and her pink lips and soft skin and go to some school I never even saw before with kids who are probably all babies anyway. I'm not a baby anymore.

"Ma, no! Please, I don't want to go on a bus! I don't need to go to school now that we're not in the old house!"

See, before we left my father and the house on Regency, before I packed my panties up and before we moved into Apartment 16 at Princess James, I was thinking I would catch the bus at the willow tree with Mary Benton and we'd take it down Brookside Drive to Cedar Grove Elementary School. Mary's still my best friend. She's 851 Regency. I'm 847. Or I was 847. Even though she's a little older than me we'd still take the bus in the morning together. I'd just come home earlier because that's what kindergarteners do in my town. They go to school for half of the day. And then I'd wait for her at the willow because second graders, which is the grade that Mary's in, come home at three o'clock. But now, with all this different stuff going on and all these forms to fill out and all the things we still need to pick up at the house on Regency I can't even think about going to school. I can't even think about it without wanting to cry.

"Mama, you do. You need to start school!" she says. She's got those tired eyes again. "You need to do this." I think about Lucy and her smooth, smooth skin and about how much I want to be like her when I grow up and about how much she does.

"Do it for me," my mother whispers and kisses me on the forehead.

This is what always happens.

Swallow and blink.

SEVEN

It's the day before the first day of Kindergarten and we are here at the Ambassador Christian Academy Church School in the basement because that's where the Kindergarten classroom is. My mother thinks it's a good idea for me to meet the teacher before the first day. "This way she knows you and you know her," she said when I was eating my Corn Pops this morning. "Trust me, in a day you'll love it."

Wrong. Just plain wrong.

Burning face and throbbing head all over again. She keeps it up. She doesn't stop. "And I know she'll love you! You can be a big helper to her, just like you are to me!"

Then she goes on about me being older for my grade, that most kids in my new class will be around five. "You're seven," she says. "Probably a whole two years older than most of the kids!"

Wrong again. I don't care what anybody says. I'm way older than seven.

My mother tells my new Kindergarten teacher she's the spitting image of Marlo Thomas. "Look at you," she says to Miss Leonard. "You're the spitting image of *That Girl* Of Marlo Thomas!"

It beats me who Marlo Thomas is or where to find *That Girl* but they don't sound like good things. My new teacher laughs, touches my mom on the shoulder and swings her head back and forth. Her brown hair swirls around the whole room like the storm cloud in *The Wizard of Oz*. But, to be fair, I guess she looks nice. Still, who cares? My father looks nice, too. Some of the time. Like when he buys me licorice on the boardwalk or takes us to Citta's for dinner. Look where that got us.

Maybe spitting image is not a bad thing to say. And maybe Marlo Thomas is movie star. Maybe Miss Leonard is the nicest person in the world. But I bet it's like the licorice and the dinner at Citta's. I bet it won't last long and soon enough Miss Leonard will be throwing mugs, knocking brand new decorations to the floor and telling me I'm no good, just like the rest of them.

* * *

Maybe I was wrong.

Kindergarten is really not so bad. I think I was too hard on Miss Leonard at first. After all, she has these skinny, long arms, kind of like Leo's, and a big smile. Yesterday, after we read *Where the Wild Things Are*, she jumped up on a desk, stretched her arms out real wide, growled like one of the wild things and asked us all if we ever felt like Max.

"C'mon, everybody!" Ms. Leonard called out to all of us. Her jean skirt was soft and light blue, and swayed all around when she hopped onto the desk. "Who in this room has ever gone to sleep at night and woke up in a dream?" Ms. Leonard's eyes opened very wide and so did everyone else's. "Or in a nightmare?" When she said "nightmare" she smiled and put her hands in front of her and wiggled her fingers so that even nightmare sounded a little silly and not scary. Most of the kids, expect for me and Willy Sanders, raised their hands to tell a story about a dream or a nightmare they had, just like Max. Willy Sanders lives in Princess James apartments, too, and he said "hi" to me once when I was playing jacks outside our door but he never talks in school. I didn't raise my hand because even though Ms. Leonard laughed when she said nightmare and tried to make it silly it made me think about how I still pee the bed. And this is a problem. For two reasons. One, I get cold. Two, I share a bed with my mom so that means not one wet nightgown, but two.

I can't believe I didn't want to come to Kindergarten because it's really fun and I have lots of jobs and what would Miss Leonard do if I wasn't here to do these jobs? What would she do?

I guess my mom was right about this. Miss Leonard lets me wheel the wagon of milk back from the kitchen to the classroom and sometimes she lets me put gold stars on the kids' papers. I told her I was also good at filling out forms.

"My mom had to fill out forms at Friendly's and Toms River Boat Works and at some big office downtown." I tell Ms. Leonard. I think back to last week, the day we went to that office, and how my mother said the word welfare the way she said the word floozy. I hate not knowing things. But the way she whispered when she said those words and the way she shook her head back and forth, back and forth, makes me believe I don't want to be involved with welfares or floozies.

"Kathy, I bet you are a big help to your mom, Sweetie. She always tells me what a good worker you are!"

I decide to tell her our good news about the food tickets.

"Guess what, Miss Leonard? After all those papers at Friendly's and the boat place and the office building she got two jobs and some tickets for us to get free food."

Ms. Leonard smiles but this time it's not a big smile, it's a little one. Looks like she needs to swallow and blink.

SUDS N DUDS

It's Saturday and my mother and I are at work, Suds N Duds Laundromat on Hooper Avenue. Her charm bracelet clinks on the countertop we use for folding clothes. It's the last load. Lots of tee shirts, tube socks, white boxers, bikini panties. And blue jeans she calls dungarees. On the sides of her fingertips dry pieces of skin stick out and sometimes catch on the stretchy tops of underwear and stockings. "God damned elastic" is what she says.

Suds N Duds is the first job my mother got after we left my father and moved into Princess James. Nobody talks about why we left. Even now, all these months later. "Enough is enough. Enough is enough." That's all anybody ever says.

When she's not at Suds and Duds my mother also takes ice cream orders at Friendly's and does the books at Toms River Boat Works. The Laundromat is my favorite, though. It's next to a pizzeria and across from a restaurant called Citta's. We used to go there sometimes when my parents were still together, before we came to live here at Princess James. Joe Citta, the guy who owns the place, knows my dad so he'd bring me extra cherries to drop into my Shirley Temples. I never ate them, just dropped them in and picked them back up again with the end of my straw. It wasn't a big deal, playing with the cherries at the table, until things got weird. That was around when my father got his hairpiece and started going out on Wednesday and Friday nights.

My mother started acting weird, too. She stopped shopping for knickknacks and headscarves and pretty aprons to wear while she cooked us dinner. She talked about a bank account for just us and sighed all the time. Hard, loud sighs. And that's also when she started yelling at me for dumb things like if we were at Citta's and I was playing with the cherries. "Don't make a mess with that, now," she'd say or, "For Chrissakes, Kathy, would you stop making messes?"

But now, here at the Laundromat, there are never messes. She lets me sit up on top of the long, silver countertops and even chew Bazooka if I want. When we work, I sit and wait for her to hand me the clean clothes that belong to Suds N Duds customers. People who drop their dirty clothes off in the morning and pick them up at five or six, all cleaned and folded. Other people, my mother calls them. She tells me it's my job to make piles—socks in one, panties in another, towels in another. Everything she gives me is folded flat. Everything smells like soap.

It's the easiest smell in the world. That's what I think.

* * *

We get home from work and sit on the couch that's also my brother's bed. We watch *Sonny and Cher*. My mother pours the same oil that we cook cutlets with into one of her hands. Then she rubs it into her fingertips. "The bleach is a bitch on my hands," she says. The oil makes her skin shine so I touch the tops of hands and press on her blue veins. They're puffy. I keep pressing and ask, "What's so big about the oil, Ma?" I push her veins and the dry pieces of skin back in and down. I want them to disappear.

I get up to change the channel.

"'Makes them soft," she says and hands me an S cookie. "Like hands should be."

Then she winks, smiles and pinches my cheek.

I plop back down onto the couch. There's nothing else on so we are back to *Sonny and Cher* which is fine with me because Cher is what my mother calls stunning. She wears lots of glittery makeup, feathers and funny outfits.

My mother's pinch doesn't really end because the oil is on my face now. I go into the bathroom, stand on the toilet seat and look into the mirror. My cheek shines just like her hands and I decide that I want to look like Cher someday. I want long hair that I can swish back over my shoulders in one move and I want smooth skin, too.

Cher's hair and her skin makes me think back to that last load of the day and those jeans, those dungarees. Before we left the Laundromat to come home tonight, when we were finishing that last load, a story came into my head about the man who wears the jeans.

I could see him. He has on a rope bracelet. The kind they sell in those Seaside surf shops at the boardwalk. He smiles. At me? Is he smiling at me? He has wavy brown hair and his sneakers are faded like the spots on the jeans. He has a backyard with grass, a little girl and a wife with a ponytail and a long skirt that ties on the side. When they go to playgrounds, and they always go to so many playgrounds, he pushes his little girl on the swings. He catches her at the bottom of giant metal slides.

"Wake up, stop dilly-dallying," my mother yelled. "C'mon this is the last load now. Almost time to go home."

I was lost. Dilly-dallying. In my story. In grass backyards. And rope bracelets and playground swings.

I never saw my father in jeans. And even though we don't live with him anymore and Jack and I only see him on Wednesday nights for early dinners and maybe on some Sunday afternoons—"Let me know if he's with some floozy," my mother mumbles as we walk out of our Princess James apartment to meet him—I am pretty sure his clothes are the same as always. No jeans, no sneakers. Just his work uniform during the day and pointy shoes at night.

My mother hands me another S cookie and pulls herself off the couch, this time she doesn't sigh, she groans. I stare at the flowers, yellow and pink zinnias, on her duster and watch her walk into the kitchen. I can't picture Cher in a duster.

I close my eyes and, in my brain, go back to work again, to the Laundromat.

I made a new pile in that last load of the day. A pile just for those jeans, those dungarees, that my mother handed to me.

And then I watched her fold a pair of panties. White, with a yellow daisy on the front.

BLACK ROAD MOVING

Here's what happened tonight. My mother was making what she sometimes calls a very sharp left but most of the time calls a bitch of a left out of the Suds N Duds parking lot and onto Hooper and I fell out of the car. I saw the black road moving. My side scraped the street and my undershirt ripped a little. I think I saw a Tastykake wrapper on the road but I'm not sure because the second after it happened my mother put the car in park, yanked me back inside and then leaned all the way over me and slammed the door shut. I said "Sorry." because how many times does she have to tell me not to lean on the door like that, for Chrissakes?

Then she put the car back in drive, handed me her handkerchief and took me to Mel's Jewelry Shop to get my ears pierced.

THE MOST BEAUTIFUL GIRL IN THE WORLD

My father's sitting in the driver's seat of his new Cadillac and Jack jumps in the front. I open the back door, get into the backseat and all I do is slide. Smooth leather and big everything.

"Don't I get a kiss?" my father says to me without turning his head. Baby purple clouds swirl into the air from his cigarette. I lean into the smoke and pull myself toward his seat. I kiss his cheek and sink into the back seat again.

It's probably our third or fourth Saturday together since they separated. My mother stands in the doorway of the apartment and waves goodbye to us. She mouths Be good. We roll away in his gigantic smoky, slippery car and I see my father take one hand off the steering wheel to push the 8-track into the deck.

"Charlie Rich. This is Charlie Rich," is what my father says at first. Then, "Don't yous wanna hear some Charlie Rich?"

All of a sudden, a weird, very low voice that sounds like it could be a cop or a school principal or something like that comes flying through the front of the car. My father has it up loud and I'm trying to stretch my neck to see Jack's face because I'd hate to be sitting up front like he is, with this loud music and my father going on and on about Charlie Rich this and Charlie Rich that.

"Let me fix these speakers, Doll," he says. His stubby fingers press and turn the radio dial. We keep floating along and Jack's just staring out the window.

Like a rocket ship Charlie Rich starts singing straight into the back of my head. He's asking if I've happened to see the most beautiful girl in the world. Actually, he's doing more than asking, he's begging. Then he asks if she was crying. My father looks into the rearview mirror and says, "See what Daddy's speakers can do?"

"It's loud," I say.

"Tell your mother I play this. Did you hear what I just said to you? Tell her I play this tape over and over."

I say okay and then hear Mr. Charlie Rich say he's sorry and that he needs his baby. We swerve into the parking lot of the Toms River Diner. Jack gets out first and runs to the door. I tuck the handkerchief my mother gave me to hold deeper into my pocket and hope we get a booth with a jukebox on the table so I can slip two quarters inside, turn the dial to Charlie Rich and find out what happens.

21st STREET

It's summer. Our new place. 21st Street in Ship Bottom, New Jersey. It's Scotty who lives near me now, not Mary Benton or Willy Sanders.

We moved here a few months ago when my parents decided to get back together. A long story, I guess, and one that really makes me mad if I spend too much time thinking about it. All I know is one minute my mother said we were taking a ride and next thing I knew we wound up here on 21st Street. It was not a long ride from the apartment, only around thirty minutes and we took the Garden State Parkway. I love the green signs on that road, reading the town names and watching the exit numbers get higher and lower.

"North higher, south lower," my mother always says. Then when we get to where we're going it never fails, she announces to no one in particular, "We reached."

They got lower when we drove here to Ship Bottom. Went from Exit 82 to Exit 63. When we pulled up to the house, which has the Barnegat Bay for a backyard and was the place my father bought and stayed in once in a while after we left 847, my mother got out of the car and walked up this tall set of stairs toward my father. He was standing on the balcony, all dressed up in a shirt that had the biggest collar I've ever seen. He had sunglasses on and was smoking his cigarette. I watched him watch her walk up those stairs. He smiled and smacked her on the butt when she got to the top. It looked like a sneaky smile if you ask me but maybe I'm not being fair.

Then I got out of the car, too, looked up at them and then out at the bay. So much water and that felt good. I heard someone say the ocean was just up the street. That we could walk there. The house was in between the bay and the ocean and I could walk to both. This helped. I'm not even sure why but knowing water is all around helped.

My father put his arm around my mother, pulling her in again, and brought her inside the house. Then a few minutes later my sisters and Jack went upstairs and then, finally, I did, too. The living room had two chairs in the shape of potato chips and everything was either orange or green. Everyone started laughing and smiling. It was all so strange and weird.

The next thing I knew we were at this restaurant called The Causeway and I was drinking Shirley Temples and eating shrimp marinara.

FLIP FLOPS AND BEAUTY MARKS

It's about a week after the Causeway and almost all our stuff is moved out of Princess James and into here.

We still have the house on Regency and Mary Benton is still there but they thought it might be good to give this a try, this new place. New leaf. That's the way everybody put it. New leaf. Fred's Texaco is still up in Toms River but my father bought an Exxon station down here so now he has two places which I guess is why all of a sudden all I hear is how important it is for Jack to act like a businessman.

Problem is he looks or acts nothing like a businessman which probably is because he's seventeen. I can say what he does look like, though. Sad and angry. That's what.

I miss Mary but there are a lot of kids on this block who are about my age. There's a girl named Angie and another girl named Lisa. My mother calls Angie's house the beet house because it's dark, dark pink. And Lisa comes from a big family with lots of boys who have short haircuts and always seem to be working in the yard. My mother calls them the Waltons.

And then there's Scotty. He's a kid in the house next door to ours who lives up north most of the time but spends summers here.

He's my favorite.

Scotty's body is nothing like mine—his legs are long sticks and his belly is tight with skin that never rolls when he sits down. A tall drink of water, is what my mother calls him.

"For Chrissakes, Scotty, Love, let me make you something to eat!" she says when he taps on the screen door and walks in at the same time. He always comes calling for me to play.

I love that Scotty is tall. I know hardly any tall people and the ones I do know are not Italian so I guess most Italian kids are short. Scotty is tall and Italian.

Our bodies are different shapes; our skin is the same. The tops of our cheeks are dark pink. Always dark pink. Maybe like Angie's house, even.

"Too much energy," my mother says. "All yous do is run around like bandits!" We both have beauty marks the exact color of Hershey's Kisses on our shoulders. We have the same white tan lines in between our first two toes from the straps of our flip-flops. On 21st St. it's either flip-flops or nothing. No laces to tie ever in the summertime here.

We taste the same, too. Scotty and me. Salty. And I only know that because of what happened in the shower.

Scotty's parents and my parents are friends now that we live here. Dotty is Scotty's mom and Dave, his dad. Because we know another Dotty (my Uncle Lou's wife, Aunt Dotty) my mother calls Scotty's mom Dottydave. Not to her face, just to us. Anyway, sometimes we all get together for dinner, especially on Friday nights. Macaroni, garlic bread and bowls of escarole salad. Maybe if Dave went clamming that week, littlenecks. The grown-ups drink wine and on some night before any food is even served, little glasses of scotch. And on those nights Scotty and I even get to drink out of the bottles of grape soda. So sweet, that soda is, even sweeter than cotton candy on the boardwalk. We eat outside under the stars next to the Barnegat Bay.

One night a few weeks ago we ate a big dinner of crabs and spaghetti. Someone had come into the station that day with a big bag of fireworks from Georgia and my father took a handful of sparklers. He gave them to us when the sun went down. Scotty said, "Man, your dad's so cool!" We ran across the dock waving them toward the boats anchored a few yards away. Music oozed from everywhere that night. My father's favorite, Sinatra, was on the transistor radio on the picnic table. I was happy for my father in that minute and that felt weird and good at the same time. Happy that Sinatra was playing and we were together and my mother's lipstick was perfect and Scotty thought my father was cool.

Then, when Scotty and I ran around the side of the house, I heard "Sunshine on My Shoulders" coming from the stereo of a blue cabin cruiser out on the bay. (My mother says John Denver is a hippie and when I asked her what that meant she didn't answer.) I even heard Springsteen that night. "Rosalita" shouted out of the old bait and tackle shop just across the cove. I'm still not sure how I heard all those songs, all those sounds. It was that kind of a night. How could it be night and still feel light? Easy. Like dancing in my yellow sundress on the counter top at Fred's Texaco.

Here's what I remember and when I do I still feel something swoosh in me and through me. I can't describe it but here's how it happened:

We keep running and chasing one another and wind up in the outdoor shower. We stand up on the bench so no one can see our feet.

"Look up," Scotty says. "The big dipper. See it?"

Why is my heart pounding? It never does this when I am with him.

"Yeah, neat," I say.

"Scotty, Scotty," Dottydave yells. She's calling for him. For us. "We got lemon ice here. Come and get it before it's all gone!"

"*Andiamo!*" I hear my mother chime in.

He steps off the bench first. Then he turns and when I jump down our shirts touch.

I laugh.

Skin. Dark pink cheeks. Salt.

The music stops. He kisses me but misses my mouth.

Grape soda on my chin.

COOL

The bunker is still frozen which is weird because it's hot as hell out here and it's been sitting on the dock for almost twenty minutes now. I go ahead and stab it with my new bait knife. It's still hard, like a rock. Cold, too, and no stinky smell yet. I'm waiting five more minutes before I cut it in half and put the tail on a line and the head in a trap. Besides, I want Scotty to come down first, before I get my traps all ready. I want him to see me cut the bunker. I want him to see how I don't even squint or turn my head when I jab the knife inside and cut it into two pieces. No chicken backs for me. That's what some people use for bait but that's for sissies. I crab with the ugliest, stinkiest bait there is. And I like it that way.

I want Scotty to think I'm cool and not afraid of things like slimy bunker and rusty crab traps. Or outdoor shower things that happen on hot nights when music is playing all over the place and we could touch the Big Dipper.

But me, sometimes I don't know what to think anymore. I know he thought it was a weird thing to happen, that kiss in the shower, because he didn't come calling for me to play for almost a whole week after that. Then when he did, it was weird. Like it was over. Like the kiss, the lemon ice, the grape soda, the Big Dipper and the outdoor shower never even happened.

Things go like that sometimes I guess.

Then after a whole week, Scotty just ran up our stairs and yelled through the screen door, "Hey, you comin out or what? I got Razzles!"

Razzles are the best so I yelled to my mom who was on the phone with the lady from JC Penney layaway, "Ma, me and Scotty are going down to the dock."

Which is where I am now. The dock. Some girls in my new class at Ethel Jacobson Elementary School were going on and on about how they hate crabbing docks because of all the splinters you get and because the way the water sometimes splashes up and gets you in the eye after boats pass by and make big waves. Then they started talking about how barnacles give them the willies. Not me. Dave told me barnacles and crabs are related, they're family. Both crustaceans.

I love crabs. I spend my days with them, catching them, measuring them, even teasing them when they sit in piles on top of one another in my basket, making bubbles and holding their little blue claws up when I poke the air above them with my tongs. When it's time to clean and then kill them I feel bad. So, I usually say a Hail Mary or an Our Father. I'm not just doing it for kicks, the killing part. It's so my mother can make her crab sauce.

When the girls in my class start getting all weird about splinters and splashes and stinky bunker I just ignore them and think about the water. And the sun. And how good of a crabber I am.

But the dock's my second favorite place. My first is the beach. The ocean. But I'm still not allowed to go there alone. I mean without a grown up. I love it there, though. It's where my mom and I go to clear our heads.

Third is the roadside place on 25th where you can get a soft vanilla cone dipped in the kind of chocolate syrup that gets hard in one second. There are picnic tables there, where people sit and eat their ice cream. And there's a small mini golf course and pinball machines too. Sometimes Scotty and me walk there, play mini-golf and Evil Knievel pinball and then buy cones that we eat on the walk home. I've only been there with Scotty. Going out for ice cream is not high on the list of favorite things for my family. Besides I think it makes my mother think about that job at Friendly's which she hated because people came in wanting too many fancy flavors.

Yesterday, Jack came out to the dock and sat on the bench behind where I pull up my lines and my traps. It's the one that Scotty carved the words SE and KP (us!) were here. At first Jack just sat there, watching me. He never does that, just sits and watches things. He's always zooming. Zooming in and out of the front door, the driveway, the station. It was kind of weird seeing him like that. Staring at me and acting all quiet.

"What are you looking at?"

"Nothing."

He had to be thinking about something. Everybody thinks about something. His eyes were bloodshot, filled to the top with water and red lines. Or maybe what I thought was water wasn't water. There were no big boats around and the bay was calm so he didn't get splashed.

Crying? Was he crying?

"Your eyes look weird," I said but felt bad right after because maybe he just wanted to sit there. Maybe he just wanted to watch me crab or look at the bay or the line that makes it hard to tell what's water and what's sky.

Maybe I hurt his feelings when I said his eyes look weird.

He sucked real hard on his cigarette. It was the first time I saw him do this and it made him look like a pro. A smoking pro. He mumbled something about being wasted. Then looked at me and said, "I got an old man. And he's up my ass." He breathed in all his snot and spit on the ground, just missing my basket.

"That's gross," I said, but then laughed. He didn't.

"Up my ass, every fucking day."

PREPARING OURSELVES

I know something for sure now: Jack gets wasted a lot.

I hear him talk about it all the time. Mostly to Bobby at the station. Bobby looks like the guy from KC and the Sunshine Band and I think he's cute but when I hear them talk about getting high, my stomach hurts.

I hate the word high.

"Stay off that shit and keep away from that Johnny Z," my mother says the second the screen door opens and the second it closes. Jack zooms. In and out.

Johnny Z's this kid who drives a yellow Trans Am and comes around the station almost every day at five o'clock. "He's good for nothing, that one," she says.

Sometimes it's hard to know what one my mother is talking about.

Like my father. She calls him one, too. "And that one, he's always crooked." Crooked is cranky and maybe that's why my father sucks in hard on his cigarette all the time. Something's always up with him. Sometimes she gives us a hint, "Prepare yourselves. He's got a bug up his ass today, so watch it!"

I don't know how I'm supposed to prepare myself for my father. Sometimes she says stuff like that but I just sit there and don't say anything because I know she worries about him and Jack and all their messes. And me asking dumb questions won't help make things better.

But I worry too.

I don't get why they have to fight all the time. I think it's about money and the station and Jack always being late to work or tired or in the place my mother calls his own frigging world.

Anyway, you don't go around sitting on dock benches, watching your little sister measure crab claws and look like you have a bucket of salty water in your eyes if you're thinking about nothing. You don't do these things if you got a clear head.

DIZZY

All the lovey-dovey stuff that went on when we first moved here to 21st Street from the apartment, that's over. My mother is back to telling my father Simmer down! all the time and my father is back to telling her You can go kiss my ass! And to all of us he just says, Yous are all alike. Or he says, Yous are all Celebres which makes no sense since Celebre is my mother's family name and we're not allowed to see them anyway. Forget the shrimp marinara, the Shirley Temples and The Causeway. Now we're just back to messes and preparing ourselves all the time.

That's why I like playing with Scotty. There's never any preparing. He's never crooked and the messes he makes are funny, not scary. Like when he sprayed his mom's new Cadillac with the garden hose when she was pulling into the driveway. He likes to ride bikes with me down to the bait shop and to the school parking lot. We play this game to see who can do more circles around the playground without getting dizzy. And he likes to crab until after dark.

So that's why I don't want that dumb kiss in the shower to go and mess everything up. I guess you could say he's my best friend now. He's the one who taught me how to suck the juice out of honeysuckles. He never wears shoes and his kneecaps stick out which Lisa from up the street says is gross but I think is neat. Nobody in my house has kneecaps that stick out. And I know for sure that nobody in my house thinks about flowers with juice inside.

FALLING FROM MY SPOT

It's the morning time that everyone calls the night and I wake up wet. Again. The back of me is cold, even up at the very top of my neck where my braids start. It's because I move around a lot when I sleep. I kick, too. That's what everyone says. And I believe them because I don't think they would lie about something like that and I even have a picture inside of my brain now, one of me swirling and kicking in my bed with my Partridge Family sheets all tangled up around my ankles.

I tilt my head down and sniff. My shoulders smell like pee. Still half asleep but even so I take off my nightgown and my wet underwear, the light blue one that has a picture of two dancing bears holding a sign that says Wednesday. Even before I put on dry pajamas I take the nightgown and the panty and roll them up into a ball with my sheets and the plastic cover for the mattress my mother bought at Bradlees last week.

"This way the mattress won't get wet if you have a little accident, Love," she said in the aisle where they sold sheets and linens.

I got mad at her because I was afraid people heard but she didn't know I was mad. I try not to let her know when that happens. She's got enough to worry about. Besides, when she calls me *Love* or *Mama* the mad doesn't last long.

I smash the big wet, smelly ball down into the dirty clothes. In my house, we don't call the white plastic hamper that holds our dirty clothes a hamper even though that's what it is. In Mary's house, they have a yellow basket in the corner of their bathroom and everybody in her family calls it a hamper. We don't. We just call it the dirty clothes.

I've seen Mary's yellow hamper a lot lately because we hang out at each other's houses all the time. We're best friends again since we are back on Regency Court and I go to Cedar Grove Elementary. That's another story about me getting mad and not showing it but it's a long one and all I really know is that last June when my brother graduated from Southern Regional High School down in Long Beach Island my parents decided it would be best if we moved back up to Toms River, back into 847 Regency. On my last day at Ethel Jacobson, I hugged my teacher and even hugged some of the girls who I still think are sissies. They gave me an Etch a Sketch as a going away present and I used it in the car on the drive back to Toms River in August. At least we got to spend the whole summer on 21st. At least I got to spend the whole summer with Scotty.

I miss him. They tell me if we keep the house on 21st that I could see him all next summer or maybe even visit his house one day during the school year. He lives up north, in Wyckoff. My mother says it's a very ritzy area. Hifalutin, she says, so I can't imagine we'll be seeing all that much of Dottydave, Dave and Scotty anymore. There's talk around here about another house my father has his eye on. It's in Beach Haven West, the town next to Ship Bottom. Why we need another house when my mother still sneaks money into her own bank account and hides the clothes we buy for ourselves confuses me but I try not to think about it all that much.

Before I go back into my room for dry pajamas I sit on the toilet and pee again. A chill goes up my back and I wake up some more. I find a washcloth, put warm water onto it, rub the bar of Ivory soap into it and clean my shoulders and down below. Down below is what my mother calls it. Every family has different words for stuff like that and I think that's funny.

I decide to go lay next to my mom. I don't do this every night, only on the nights that I wake up wet. When I was really little I slept next to her all the time because we shared a bed in the apartment and also because I got scared a lot. Like when I spent a week being terrified because of a picture I could not push out of my mind. This happened when Jack came home from the drive-in and kept going on and on about how the girl in the movie had green eyes and a head that spun around.

Now it's only once in a while that I need to lie down next to her at night. It's only once in a while that I pee the bed. I think the last time was four nights ago, on Sunday. I woke up, dried myself off and got into their bed. My father was snoring and he was on his back with his hands folded high on his stomach. I thought it looked so weird and I got spooked when I saw his hands go up and down each time he snored. He looked the way Grandpa Jack looked at his wake—totally still, folded hands on his stomach, eyes shut. No different. Except Grandpa Jack was dead.

I sat on my mother's side of the bed and tried to lie down fast but easy, too. I didn't want to wake her. I only wanted her to pull me in tight so that I wouldn't feel like I was falling off. Whenever my mother pulls me close to her on her side of the bed her skin is right on mine and it's smooth and smells like the beach. She has some tiny brown spots on her arm—she says they're from the sun but she doesn't care.

"I don't care about these spots, sun spots they call them. The sun is my medicine!"

I counted those spots the other night when I tried falling back to sleep. I stopped at twenty but I don't care about them either. Sun spots are the least of our worries.

So now I tiptoe down our short hallway, walk into their room and stop short. I freeze. Rock solid like my frozen bunker. I don't move. I can't. All I can do is I see what I see.

My mother lies on her stomach. I never saw her like this before. All the other times I went in she was on her side. All the other times I went in I could always see her face, sleepy, shiny, too, from Vaseline. And that funny satin cap she wears to bed to "keep my hair nice at night," she says. But now she's on her stomach and I don't see the cap anywhere. Her hair is all messy and I see bobby pins on the table next to the bed. She's wearing something very fancy. Something fancy and weird. Something like what they sell at Frederick's of Hollywood, that place in the mall that makes Mary and me giggle and speed up when we walk by.

The thing my mother's wearing has lots of lace on it and it's pink. And it's not where it is supposed to be, this nightgown or pajama top or whatever it is. It's way up high, scrunched up to almost where her boobs are and her butt is right there out in the open! No covers, no sheet, no nightgown, no tee shirt. The only thing on her butt is my father's hand.

They are both asleep and I still don't know what to do. I feel like I'm going to be sick but I can't move. I just keep looking at her butt and his hand. I've seen her with no clothes on before so I can't understand why I feel the way I do right now. Her butt is rounder than I remember it and it seems like it would be mushy if I were the one touching it. But I'm not the one touching it.

He is.

The color bothers me. It's very white, like whipped cream that comes in a can. Now I really feel sick because I love whipped cream and I don't want to be thinking about it right now. In this moment. In this room. Seeing what I am seeing.

Maybe it looks whiter than it really is because his hand is tan. But then I think about the broken cars, about the station and the gas pumps. Maybe his hand isn't tan. Maybe it's just dirty.

And then I get even more confused and sick to my stomach. Because in that moment I can't decide if I hate my father for touching her like that or if I feel bad for him.

* * *

One of my chores on Saturday mornings is to clean our bathrooms. I always have to rub his bathroom mirror extra hard with the paper towels and Windex. The little dried beads of soap are hard to get off. I never knew how they got there until I watched him scrub his hands one night after work. He rubbed the fingernail brush so hard across his hands and the tips of his fingers that the little soapy bubbles flew off of the brush and on to the mirror. And that's where they stayed until my Saturday morning chores. Now it makes me wonder if that scrubbing is all for nothing.

I wonder if he'll ever get his hands clean.

But, still, how could she let him do this to her? She's always talking about how he'll never change and I heard her call him a son of a bitch bastard last week at the beauty parlor. I was sweeping the hair clippings from the floor with the broom because Jim says I'm his Saturday afternoon sweeper, his Saturday afternoon girl. Anyway, I heard Jim say, "Catherine, how's your old man? How's Freddy?" He spun her around and gave her a big fancy mirror to hold so she could get a good look at the back of her beehive. I wasn't able to hear her whole answer but I swear to God I think she called my father a son of a bitch bastard.

And now look at her. Lying right there in my spot wearing this weird lace getup and letting him put his hand all over her mushy white butt.

WAITING BY WINDOWS I

"Go wait by the door and watch from the window, Love," my mother says to me. "Tell me when Daddy's car pulls up so I can put the macaroni in."

"Ok, Ma," I say.

I finished my spelling words, did all my math homework and set the table already. I've got nothing better to do. So, I walk over to the front door and wait by the window for my father's car to pull up.

We have two front doors, one that's made of wood and one that's made of metal. The wood one stays open all the time, except for when we go to bed at night or when there's a big fight and somebody slams it. Fights, they happen almost every day now and they're getting bigger, too. And louder.

Sometimes it starts with the shit my brother is taking and ends with my mother's family.

My mother to Jack: Watch yourself with that shit. Straighten out. Staying away from those troublemakers. Screwing your head on straight.

My father to us all: Go back where you came from. Go fuck yourselves, all of you. Yous are all alike.

Or sometimes it starts with my mother being late to the station to bring the deposit slips back and ends with her getting her hair done the way my father doesn't like it—in a bouffant, instead of the way prefers, in a beehive.

When big fights happen the walls of our house shake. Once the shaking even knocked over the candy dish from the table in the front hall. Black licorice bits were everywhere and one even got stuck in the white lines in between the tile. That's because somebody stepped on it after the dish fell and now there's a black mark there that won't go away. Anyway, the metal door has a screen we put into it when summer starts so we can get fresh air.

"Fresh air and sunshine, the best medicine there is!" my mother says. Sometimes she changes fresh air to "salt air" or "ocean air." That's when I get even more in the mood for summer. Crabbing. Flip flops. Scotty.

I like when the screen part gets put in and the glass part goes in the basement for the season. That's when the door is a lot easier to open, it's always warm outside, and I can hear when Mary and Kim are walking up our driveway to come get me to play. Kim lives on Castle, the street next to ours, and she's our friend now, too.

But sometimes it means the wooden one gets closed, especially lately with everything going on around here between the shit my brother takes and my mother's hairstyles.

It's not summer yet, though, it's March 19th, and so I'm looking through glass not screen. I know for sure it's March 19th because my mother bought the special March 19th pastry for dessert. It's St. Joseph's Day. He's the saint for fathers and workers. So even though my father never goes to church like my mom and me do, he still gets to eat the special *zeppoles* after dinner. It figures. I guess you don't have to go to church to eat the *zeppoles*. Maybe you just have to be a father or a worker.

The glass is a little wet because it's so cold outside and inside it's warm. It gets like that when my mother has water boiling and the oven is on. I make swirls with my finger on the window. Then I write KP+SE with a heart around it.

I watch and wait for my father's car to pull up. And when it does I'll tell her she can put the macaroni into the pot.

GOOD FRIDAY

It's Good Friday so I'm off from school. Lucy, Ria, my mother and I are walking on the beach in Seaside Park because we got everything done. We dyed the eggs, ironed our dresses and sliced the pepperoni for the special *frittata* my mother makes, only for Easter.

"I'm going to see if he'll let me go see Grams tomorrow," she says to them but I bet nobody thinks I'm listening. They never think I listen.

I walk behind, looking for clamshells. Dumb idea. Way too early for them. Lots of driftwood and beer bottles, though. The sand feels warmer than usual for this time of year. My toes sink in deep and I wish for summertime.

My father's going to make a mess if she asks to do what she's not allowed to do. I forgot about my toes and about summer and just get worried.

* * *

"What are you, crazy?" my father screams.

Why is she bringing this up at dinner now? He's crooked to begin with.

All she made tonight was *pasta fagioli* and English muffin pizzas. Good Friday, no meat. "You got another thing coming if you think you're going to walk into that house and wish them a Happy Easter. They don't give a shit about you."

His eyes burn. His cigarette does too.

"But, Freddy, I won't stay long. Please don't make a mess now."

With her *moppina* she wipes a wet lump of gravy from the plastic Easter tablecloth. Her forehead's shiny so she wipes that too.

Then she pours him some more root beer.

"Forget it. You're not going."

He points his finger in her face. "And don't let me find out you go, because so help me, if I do, there'll be trouble."

I get up, put my dish in the sink and start to cry.

"And you," he yells at me, "don't start."

He flicks his cigarette ash in the black ashtray with Mt. Airy Lodge written in gold on the inside. We got to go there because my father worked like a dog last year and sometimes he wins trips from this fancy tire company. Once we went to the Bahamas. My brother teased me the whole drive home from Mt. Airy Lodge because I kept looking through the back window of our Cadillac, afraid we'd get pulled over and arrested. I hate when we go places and my mother takes the towels and ashtrays.

EASTER SUNDAY

It's Easter morning and I wake up to my father asking my mother another question she knows not to answer: "What the hell kind of a woman are you?"

Happy Easter.

He goes on. "They hate me and think I'm a no good *stunad*. You want to see them bastards when they think I'm shit?"

On the way into the living room to see "if the Easter Bunny came" I wish there really was an Easter Bunny. One hop into this house and he'd change everything. I didn't even try to make myself smile when I got to the living room and saw the yellow and pink basket on the coffee table. My mother was still in the kitchen with my father. Words zoom from one room to another. Words that seem all wrong. Tramp. Bitch. Whore.

I hate when this happens. I hate when he happens.

My Easter treats sit waiting for me: on top of a small bump of plastic green grass are Peeps, a chocolate duckling, a bag of jellybeans and a candy cross.

I hear the phone ring and my father's hard footsteps heading down the hall. Their bedroom door slams. The phone stops ringing and my mother leans into the opening between the kitchen and the living room. Her face looks like she has a fever and her hair looks like she got caught in a tornado. "Get dressed. We're going to mass."

We're at ten o'clock mass at St. Joseph's Church on Hooper Avenue. She wants to be home by noon to put the lasagna in the oven so that it'll cook slow and all the way through. Once there was a big mess because she put the lasagna on the table and the inside was still cold. When we step out of the pew I see her wipe her eyes. I don't ask, "What's the matter?" I just take the quarter she hands me. Her fingernails still have the frosty white nail polish on from when I painted them a few nights ago.

"Go light a candle," she says. "Go say a prayer."

"What prayer?" I hope she doesn't say the Apostles' Creed because I never remember the words.

"Pray for patience," she mumbles and blows her nose.

I drop the coin into the brown metal box, take one of the skinny wooden sticks from the box of sand and light it from one of the red candles that's already burning. There's one unlit candle left in the top row. I light it, then push the burning stick back in the sand. My favorite part: putting out the fire. I kneel down on the velvet pad at the bottom of the prayer stand and stare at the candle flames. My dress itches already, the slip underneath is too tight. It rubs against my skin.

I ask God for two things: patience and hot lasagna.

TWELVE STREET AND CRUMB

Sometimes when my mother has it up to here with Grandma Lucy, my father's mother, she calls her *Crumb*. Not to her face, only to our faces and some other people's faces, but that's what she calls her. *Crumb*.

"So help me God," my mother said to Aunt Terri when she was on the phone with her a few months ago. She was stuffing green peppers and her hands had big globs of rice and meat on them so I had to hold the phone by her ear. "Terri, I'm telling you I saw her glom two anisette cookies off of that table and stick them right in her duster pockets! I'll be goddamned."

I thought she was done talking about Grandma Lucy stealing the anisette cookies but then she said, "What am I, an idiot? Right from the frigging table, for cryin' out loud. She's such a crumb, that one!"

Then after that she said, "Terri, I'm making stuffed peppers for Charlie down the street. Cataract surgery. I gotta go." So I took the receiver away from her ear, unhooked its cord from the hanging part on the wall and then let it twirl all around until there were no kinks left. Then I hung it back up. Nobody else in this house ever does this so if it wasn't for me the phone cord in the kitchen would probably be all knotted up twenty-four hours a day, seven days a week. I bet nobody ever thinks about that.

Crumb is not even her best one. I swear to God we have these cousins or friends from up north, around by Roselle Park or Newark Airport. I'm not sure we're really related by blood, kind of like the way we are with Aunt Terri and Uncle John who are my godparents. These people are *paisans* like my father says, but all my life I never heard my mother call them anything but *Twelve Street*. She probably means Twelfth Street but it always comes out Twelve Street and that's what she calls the whole family. And now that's what we call them, too. But not to their faces, either. I know they have their own regular names but as crazy as it sounds I only know one of them. Josephine. Josephine Lombardi. My mother says Josephine has a heart of gold and has a cross to bear with that sister of hers. I don't know the sister's name, though. Josephine with the golden heart and the cross is the only name I know and, as far as I'm concerned, everybody else is just *Twelve Street*.

Lots of times when Twelve Street comes down to the shore from up north they come to our house first, before going over to Seaside. My mother usually makes chicken cutlets, fried peppers and tomato salad. She tells them they should put something in their stomachs before going to the beach. Lots of times she calls my father at the station to tell him to come home for lunch and to say hello because Twelve Street is stopping by. I think he likes to come home when company is over in the middle of the day. It's mostly in the summer when that happens. Nobody I know from North Jersey goes to the beach in the winter.

"And, Freddy, bring some quarters home so they don't have to walk all over God's creation trying to make change for the meters."

I was thinking about this the other day in church. About how sometimes my mom calls Grandma Lucy *Crumb* behind her back but at the same time how she makes her bouillon after she gets her gums scraped by Dr. Pirraglia and how if we're out shopping and Grandma Lucy is with us she rushes her home so she can watch her stories. I was thinking about this because the priest was talking about how good people make mistakes and about how we need to ask for forgiveness. I am pretty sure Grandma Lucy doesn't know my mom calls her *Crumb* but if she did I think she'd forgive her but she probably wouldn't stop putting cookies in her duster pockets. I even think Twelve Street would laugh if they knew that's what my mom called them.

Or at least Josephine Lombardi would. I know that. It's the sister I'm worried about.

WEDNESDAY NIGHT FISH FRY

It's another Wednesday night and my mom and I are going back and forth about dinner. About where to go. Since it's Wednesday night we're going out. That much is true. That's for sure. I decide I feel more like pancakes than fish fry.

"Ma, Ground Round or the diner?" I ask and plop into the passenger seat. (I say plop all the time now because that's what my mom says I do. "Be careful the way you sit. You just plop yourself down like a truck driver. C'mon, sit like a lady!" Besides, I like the way the word sounds. Plop!) The leather is hot on my skin—especially my butt—so I rock back and forth to get used to it. The Ground Round is this restaurant over on Hooper that has a special Wednesday Night Fish Fry thing. I think they make such a big deal about it because you get a whole dinner for a really cheap price. They put baskets of peanuts on all the tables and you can throw the shells on the floor. We go there a lot because I love how it feels to throw shells on the ground without getting yelled at. I also love that they play music very loud. The last time we went they played music from *Saturday Night Fever* which, of course, I didn't see thanks to Nancy Jenkins, the shampoo girl at Joel Richards. She told my mother there's a lot of cursing and there's a scene that takes place in the back seat of a car where a girl touches some guy's crotch.

My mother likes The Ground Round, too, but sometimes she says she doesn't have the head for that place because she sees everybody and their brother there.

But I really want to go to the Toms River Diner tonight instead of The Ground Round. Ordering pancakes or two eggs over light with toast and jelly for dinner always makes us laugh. And my mother has that weird look lately. Like there's some trouble going around. Like it would be good if she laughed. Besides the diner is right around the corner from St. Joe's and I have a feeling that she's going to want to stop by after we eat so we can light a candle and pray.

But first, pancakes for dinner at the diner.

CROOKED

We're in the fifth pew, me rubbing my fingers over the soft, fuzzy lines on my new brown corduroys and my mother rubbing hers over the beads of her rosary. I flip through the pages of the missal. Why are the pages in church books so thin? They feel like tissue paper. Nothing like the pages in the book I am reading now about a half-Jewish girl named Margaret who's waiting for her boobs to grow. My mother kneels on the pillow thing that everybody kneels on in church when something important is about to happen and puts her head into her hands. She presses her fingers into her forehead hard. I hate when she does this. I mean I hate the way it makes her look. Sad is not even close to describing it. She looks like a hundred times worse than sad.

I lean over and whisper in her ear, "Ma, when can we go?" The spritzes of Charlie she sprayed on the back of her neck from the tester bottle in the drug store are not as strong smelling now like they were when she first sprayed it, but I still get a whiff of it when my nose touches her neck. We stopped at Towne Pharmacy after our pancakes and before church to pick up aspirin and this weird stuff in a blue bottle called Brioschi. My father always takes it when he eats too fast and gets *agita* and he told her before he left to go play cards with his *paisans* that he had no more Brioschi left. When we walked past the perfume aisle my mother spritzed on Charlie and I spritzed on Wind Song. My mother never passes a tester bottle without spritzing. "It's important to smell nice," she reminds me. "Remember that."

She always talks about smelling nice.

The back doors of the church open and Mr. Ginesco walks in. He owns a gas station, too, just like my father, but it's all the way on the other side of town and it's Getty not Texaco. He's at church a lot. We always see him here. He's one of the guys who pull the long basket in and out of the pews so that people can put money into it. My mother never forgets to tell my father how she saw Gerry Ginesco at church.

I whisper again, "Ma, c'mon, I wanna go." Her head is still resting in her hands. She tucks her rosary beads back into the zipper part of her pocketbook and shakes her head back and forth. "Dear, God, give me strength," she says.

I pray too. Dear God, I hope he's not crooked this week.

My mother spends a lot of time thinking about who's crooked and who's not. Lots of times she'll says things like, "Watch yourself, he's crooked tonight!" Or if I come home from a crummy day at school she'll say something like, "Ok, what's with the puss? What are you crooked for?"

But usually she's talking about my father because I don't get crooked very much.

THAT SHIT

I need one tube sock for Mrs. Perry's the big end-of-the year Social Studies project. Mine's on the history of puppets. So now I have to make a puppet from the olden days which really stinks because even though it's only April it feels like summer outside and I'm stuck in here, in this house, worrying about tube socks.

The phone rings so I get it. Grandma Lucy. When she asks what I am doing inside on such a nice day I tell her I am working on a big school project.

"Why the hell do they give you kids so many projects? It's for the birds, I'll tell you. School today? It's for the birds."

Grandma Lucy has a whole list of things that are for the birds: school, Alice Cooper, my father's hairpiece and people who are so busy they can't pass a dust rag over their furniture every once in a while.

"Beats me," I tell her. After I hang up the phone I go into Jack's room to find a spare sock. He wears tube socks so I know one will be in there.

But first I find the stuff. I know it's what my mother now calls *that shit*. It's deep in his sock and underwear drawer under a small stack of filthy, folded up papers and matchbooks. I can't believe he keeps this gross stuff right next to his underwear.

Disgusting. Absolutely disgusting.

It smells weird even though the bag it's in is all tight, rolled up a bunch of times from the top. It still smells. Right through the bag. What's inside looks like the spice my mother puts on sausage stew. Oregano, I think it is. Or maybe basil.

* * *

I remember last Wednesday night.

My father was at his Rotary Club meeting. Apparently, that's what important businesspeople do, they join The Rotary Club and go to meetings. I was waiting for my mother on the front stoop because we were going to go to K-Mart to look at the new bathing suits that had just arrived according to the coupon thing we got in the middle of the newspaper. I was holding her pocketbook on top of my knees and jingled the car keys around my finger. All ready to go, like she told me to get.

"I'll be right out," she said after I put my jacket on and walked toward the front door. "I just want to get the last load out of the dryer before we leave. That's all we need! I got enough to worry about without having a pile of wrinkled clothes to deal with."

Worry. Always worry.

"Go. Sit outside," she said. Go get my pocketbook and my keys and wait for Mommy outside."

The clinking and jingling of the car keys wasn't loud enough to cover their voices. Probably because Jack's room is the first one on the left, his window faces our front yard. It was hard not to hear them in his room. I'd be lying if I said I tried not to hear.

I never really try not to hear.

Because the truth is that I just want to know what's going on. Why always worry? Why always fights and messes?

My mother yelled something to Jack about not getting involved with that shit. Then she said she saw that shit in his drawer and that he better stay away from that shit and stay away from Kenny up the street, too. "He's frigging trouble, I'm telling you. You mark my word!" she said in a yell-whisper. Then I heard him say, "Catherine, ease up would you!" My brother started calling my parents Catherine and Fred about three years ago and I'm used to it now but all my friends think it is the weirdest thing they ever heard.

"Watch yourself, Mister."

Then a door slammed. I bet he slammed it because my mother hates closed doors. The next thing I knew we were backing out of the driveway and she was saying how he better take it easy and use his head or he'll be sorry.

Then she asked me what color bathing suit did I think I wanted to get this year.

*　*　*

I grab a blue and white sock out of its drawer. My hands shake. I shuffle the papers and the matches back into their spots so everything looks like it did when I first opened my brother's sock and underwear drawer.

THAT SHIT, PLUS MORE

It's a week after I hand in the project and I'm glad that's over. I worked so hard on it. Even my father noticed.

"Must be some important puppet you got there, Doll," he said the other night when he was shining his shoes. He huffed a little when he said it because bending down and rubbing the brush back and forth isn't so easy.

I'm in the yard with the willow tree, the yard that separates my house from Mary's. It's Mary, Beth, Dawn and me and we're playing catch with a beanbag. I miss it and it lands smack on the seat of Jack's Camaro because when he came home from work an hour ago he parked in the driveway and left his T tops off. Everyone on the block always knows it's him coming home from work. They hear him from down the street. The souped-up engine. That stereo system. Besides he drives like a bat out of hell. That's what Mr. Sheffield says. The Sheffields live in the house across the street but I've only been inside once. My mother says they keep it like a museum.

"I'll be goddamned," my mother usually says when she hears Jack pulling his car into the driveway. "When will he learn?" Then the usual shaking of her head, maybe a long sigh and she might end with, "When I'm pushing daisies, that's when he'll listen to me!"

Beth picks dandelions and lines them up on the grass. "Why does your brother always play that stupid song every night when he comes home from the station?" she asks. Her freckles are so pink and they seem to grow by the minute. She stops with the dandelions and starts biting her fingernails instead.

"Because it's cool, that's why!" Dawn snaps back. She puts her hand on her hip and tries to act cool. Everyone knows Dawn's in love with Jack, it's the biggest crush she ever had. Beth told me once that Dawn said she thought Jack and her would go good together because they both had brown eyes and black hair. Beth also said that Dawn carved JP and DS on the willow. "My cousin, Ricky, listens to 'Free Bird,' too," she brags. "He says Skynard rules!" She cracks her Bazooka and rubs lip gloss onto her lips for the tenth time. For one second, the whole world smells like green apples.

I lean over the top of the car door and try to act like a big shot by reaching for the beanbag without opening the door. Kind of like the California girls on TV who hop into convertibles instead of using the doors. My stomach touches the fuzzy, rubber pieces that the window slides in and out of and it tickles. I am careful that the button on my jean shorts doesn't rub against the shiny black paint because that's all we need. A scratch on his precious car. I think he loves his car more than anything else in the world.

I smell it again. That smell. That shit.

I toss the beanbag over my head and behind me hoping it lands in the bushes and Mary, Beth and Dawn will have to go find it. It does and I'm glad. Right in the prickly bush next to the magnolia tree.

"Hey, what's the big idea!" Mary yells and they race over to look for it.

I open the compartment in the middle of the seats. This is where most people keep tissues, 8- tracks and sucking candies. That's when I see the same stuff again. That shit. Two Ziploc bags full.

And more. A tiny bottle of eye drops and a weirdo thing that looks like my sister's tweezer but has a feather on one end and ridges on the other. I grab one bag and shove it down my shorts. The bag I took was covering something else, though. Something on the bottom of the compartment.

* * *

It's a small jar, about the size of a crab claw, with a black cap. It's the bronze and copper colored and when I look through the glass I see there is something white and powdery inside. It looks like something scientists use.

But it's not. That much I know. Jack's no scientist.

I shut the top of the compartment and wonder if my mother calls what's inside the jar shit, too. Definitely not oregano.

* * *

It wasn't easy shoving the bag down my shorts because they're pretty tight on me. This is probably why my mother said we need to start watching ourselves because being chunky runs in the family. On both sides. I hop off the top of the door and run toward the house.

"I gotta go, you guys," I yell to them. All I see are their butts because their heads are under the bushes looking for the beanbag. "I need to set the table."

The bag is sticking to the elastic on the top part of my panties and it pinches me.

Dawn crawls out from the bushes first and yells to me, "See 'ya. Tell Jack I said hi." Then she screams to the two butts, "C'mon you freaks, race 'ya!"

"No, tell him Mary wants to have his babies!" I hear Beth snap back. The screen door slams behind me. I look back and see them race to the willow.

THE ANSWER

His chest is moving, no doubt about it.

Up. Down. Up. Down.

It's Day Two at Uncle Johnny's wake. I spent all day yesterday looking at his chest and I swear to God it moved then and it's moving now. And this is not the first time this has happened to me. It's not the first time I've been at a wake and would bet one Bazooka and five watermelon Jolly Ranchers that the person in the coffin is still breathing.

"It looks like he's breathing. Like he's still alive," I say to Grandma Lucy. Uncle Johnny is Grandma Lucy's brother so she gets to sit in the front row.

"Body might be dead, Kathy, but the soul's still alive," she says to me. "My kid brother, Johnny," she mumbles to no one in particular. Then she takes her shaky hand, cups it, kisses her thumb and pointer finger, makes a sign of the cross and presses her hand to her heart. When she does this, and she does this all the time but not just at wakes, I notice how thin her skin is and how flimsy her veins look underneath. It's hard not to notice that.

"God rest his soul," she whispers.

This is about the ninety-ninth time in the last twenty-four hours that someone has told me that Uncle Johnny's soul's alive. It still doesn't answer my question about the moving chest.

Why should wakes be any different than anyplace else? And it's not just lately. It's been like this forever. No matter where we are or what we are doing, nobody wants to answer my questions. I hate being the youngest in the family. It stinks. And it's even worse when people call me the baby.

The flowers that people sent to Uncle Johnny are being held up by metal rods that stand straight and tall. They remind me of the camera stands the people who come to take school pictures use. On both sides of the casket, there are flower arrangements shaped like hearts and crosses with gold cardboard letters splattered across the fronts, spelling out things like Beloved Uncle and Rest in Peace. One of the arrangements is so big it looks like something from the Mummers Parade. I only know this because we watch this strange parade every New Year's Day. It's only on the Philly station. Anyway, one particular arrangement for Uncle Johnny looks like it's made of thousands of red roses smashed up, one against the other. The fancy gold writing splashed over its center says, Knock 'Em Dead, Johnny Boy. Curly red velvet ribbons fall to the floor from the loops on the *J* in Johnny and the *o* in Boy.

Knock 'em dead? A little late, don't you think? I could be a smart aleck right now and say something my mother would call fresh but decide that would be mean and I don't want to start any trouble.

"Who sent that one, Ma?" I ask. I saw the funeral home guy carry it into the viewing room a few minutes ago but didn't know what it said until right now, until he turned it around so that it faced out to the crowd. When he walked through the door people oohed and aahed and, at first, I thought that was because he looked like Donny Osmond. Big brown eyes and slick hair. But he was smiling a big wide smile, which I thought was a really dumb thing to be doing at the time.

"Holy Mother of God," my mother whispers back to me, shaking her head and making a quieter version of her usual clicking noises that happen when she sees something she might call utterly ridiculous or absolutely unnecessary. "Must have cost a fortune!"

Another unanswered question. So, I vow to figure it out and give myself a due date—a day and a half. The project makes me feel better and gives me something else to do with my time. So, I decide this: By the time Uncle Johnny's coffin gets to the cemetery and is propped up on that big steel holder, just long enough for everybody to say their last prayers and their last goodbyes and toss their red, pink or white carnations onto the top, I'll know who sent the glitzy flowers.

* * *

Finally, the last hour of the two-day wake. My cheeks are sore from people who I haven't seen in a while squeezing them and the elastic on the leg holes of my panty itches because it's not covered in cotton. I had to wear the fancy panties (which are slippery but itchy, too) so my dress would not stick to me when I walk. I'm sitting in the second row, sucking on my fifth butterscotch candy and watching my cousin Nadia, who sits next to me, flip through the pages of the Guest Book.

My father is a few feet away talking to Salvatore and Massimo, two of his third cousins.

"Traffic was a bitch on the turnpike," Massimo says. From my eavesdropping, I learn that they traveled all the way from Down Neck Newark to pay their respects. I hear that expression a lot. Down Neck Newark. It's the neighborhood my family lived in before they moved an hour south, to the Shore. It's where my father was born and also where my sisters and brother, Lucy, Jack and Ria, were born. I am the only one born a few miles from the ocean and I like to think that's why I love the beach as much as I do. More than anyone else. I like to think that makes me special.

Who doesn't want to be special?

My mother was born in Brooklyn, but her family moved to Newark at some point and that's where my parents met. I have to say I really don't like thinking about that, about them on a date or hanging out at each other's house as teenagers. Forget thinking about them kissing or any stuff like that. It's a weird picture and not the kind I want popping into my head. And it was a thousand times worse on that night back when I was still wetting the bed and I saw them asleep in their bed, his hand where it shouldn't have been.

So, in the middle of Salvatore and Massimo talking about traffic and who knows what else to my father, I see another cousin come up to them and pat them all on their backs. He goes on to say that a bunch of Uncle Johnny's *paisans* who he played cards with every Friday night for the past thirty years sent the fancy flowers. Some friends!

I knew I'd get my answer, though.

POOR JESSICA SMITH

This may be Uncle Johnny's first wake (as a dead person) but it's my fourteenth. A few years ago, maybe I was about eight or nine, my parents dragged me to what felt like three wakes in one month. For weeks on end all my mother said was, "It always happens like that. That's what they say. Threes! Death comes in threes!"

Last week, in the cafeteria at lunch, Joey Rodolfo told a bunch of us that he heard the lunch lady, Mrs. Kaye, was absent because her husband died. That got us into a conversation about dying and wakes and I come to find out that some of my friends have never even been to a wake.

"Still not allowed," Jessica Smith said when I asked her why.

"Not allowed?" I asked. It was the craziest thing I ever heard.

* * *

I was never "not allowed" to go to a wake. Jessica Smith said something about her parents thinking it could cause nightmares but I never remember hearing my parents talk about whether I was old enough or if it was a good idea or if it would cause nightmares. If someone died, the Pontoriero family went to pay their respects.

Because it's the right thing to do.

And, if for some reason or another, my mother and father were thinking twice about whether they needed to go, whether they were obligated or not, then a trip up the attic stairs would solve that problem.

Not always, but most of the time this is how it might go: My mother might press hard on the first step of the shaky ladder with her bare foot, while my father climbed up the stairs, all the time making coughing and loud breathing noises. "Careful, Freddy, please. All we need now is for you to fall," she'd probably say. My father would get to the top of the ladder stairs and then step onto the wood that we're supposed to step on when we're in the attic so that we don't fall through the ceiling. (I learned this last year when my mother said I was old enough to go up into the attic and help take down the Christmas decorations.) Once up there my father might find the milk crate which held the Guest Book that was signed by every single person who came to my Grandpa Jack's wake years before. (Grandpa Jack was my Grandma's Lucy's husband and my father's father.) It even has the signatures of the people who got kicked out (by my father) for one reason or another over the course of the two days.

"If they came for Pop," he might say, "then we need to go. Not for nothing, Catherine, but it's only right." He might shake his head, he might rub his hands across his forehead or his jaw. He might look like a guy who just wants people to know he's got some good inside of him. "I got to show my face," he might say.

Then my mother might say, after her long, hard sigh (depending on how well we know the person) "Alright then. We'll go. I'll get your dark suit out and iron your shirt."

She might ask me to go get her black cape in the cedar closet and then she might say, "I hope to dear God it doesn't smell like moth balls."

* * *

Since the wake is almost over I go up to Tony Boy, one of my other cousins, to see how many butts with lipstick he's found since yesterday morning. This is a game my cousins and I play at wakes. Who could find the most cigarette butts that have lipstick on the ends is the winner, but there's no official winner because you could say you found thirteen and really only found three and nobody would know. So, it's kind of a joke. But whoever does say the most gets to take five prayer cards from each of the other players. The prayer cards are usually in stacks next to the Guest Book. They have a prayer, plus the dead person's name, birthday and day that they died written on one side and a picture of the Virgin Mother or of Jesus or a sunset or a waterfall on the other. Everybody has to fork up their prayer cards and hand them over to the person who finds the most butts with lipstick.

I started the night with eighteen prayer cards and hope to add to my stack.

Tony Boy says he found ten. Nadia, seven. Gloria, twelve. I only found six but I say eight. Gloria wins. She smiles and cracks her gum when we each hand her five of our prayer cards and all I can think of is poor Jessica Smith.

She doesn't even have one.

THE BLIZZARD OF '78: NOW WHAT?

"Oh, Madonna look at it out there! A frigging blizzard for God's sake!" my father says pushing open the front door.

"Jesus, Freddy, it's really coming down," my mother says.

I watch them from the end of the short hallway. The wind makes the bottom of her blue velour robe sway and rub across her ankles. After he closes the door, he wipes off the snowflakes that blew in and landed on her shoulders and her hair. They stand next to one another and look at the snow through the glass on the storm door. They look different from this view. I can't explain how. They just look different.

Jim had done a beehive last Saturday and it needed to last her the whole week. "Do it tight, Jim, I got a busy week. I'm all over God's creation this week," I heard her say to him when I was sweeping up all different colors and lengths of hair from the floor at Joel Richards.

My mother turns away from him and the door and says, "I need to get to the A&P before it gets any worse. I need to pick up some things. Today's a good soup day. I'll make a nice pot of vegetable beef soup."

We all walk back into the kitchen and my mother pours my father his coffee. I sit down and eat my Quisp and try to figure out the answers to the riddles on the side of the box. My father puts the milk in his coffee and stirs it hard and fast. The spoon clinks on the inside of the cup. Some mornings I hear his clinking spoon from my bedroom and that's how I knew it was time to get up for school and that my father is leaving for work soon. He likes to get to the station early, do his book-work and get ready for his customers. When they start coming in, he starts fixing their cars.

"Are you nuts?" my father blurts. He smells like cigarettes. "You can't drive in this weather!" He zipped up his jacket and blew his nose into the navy blue bandana he keeps in his back pocket. "I'm closing the shop today, nobody's coming out in this weather. Just gimme a list. I'll go. And, you," he says and points to me. "You go get dressed. You're coming with me."

Everything stops. Everything stands still. Frozen and silent.

My father and I never go anywhere together, just the two of us. It's always my mom and me. Frick and frack, she calls us. I think back to Princess James and how we went everywhere together. I even remember us saying that a singer named Helen Reddy sang a song on the radio just for us. "You and Me Against the World." That's what it felt like then. And sometimes still does.

Now what? My father and me. Alone. I have nothing to say to him if other people are not around. The radio announcers and television guys are going on and on about how this blizzard, the Blizzard of '78, they are calling it, could be the worst one that has hit in decades. The shiver in me has nothing to do with the snow. It comes from the place where worry grows. I imagine us alone in the car. I imagine the silence. His cigarettes. The sound of my gum cracking.

Swallow and blink.

THE BLIZZARD OF '78:
GROCERY-SHOPPING DADDY

I am eleven and this is the first time, ever, that I see my father in a grocery store. I heard stories from my mother about when I was a little baby he sometimes picked up formula or diaper pins on his way home from work but I never really believed her. I just thought it was another one of those stories that, on good days, made him out to be someone he really wasn't. Some grocery-shopping Daddy who wore faded blue jeans, listened to rock and roll music and read me Dr. Seuss books at bedtime. The father I know wears a work uniform and shines his shoes at night. He listens to Sinatra and Jerry Vale and reads only the *Asbury Park Press*, and that doesn't happen at bedtime. It happens at dinnertime.

And now here we are. Buying soup stuff together at the A&P during the Blizzard of '78. I'm wheeling the cart up and down the empty aisles and he's shuffling around looking like he's lost in China or Africa or some other faraway place. But something happens and his weird look fades. His face changes. I think it gets brighter. He looks happy.

The snow is coming down harder and harder but it's not mattering to him. Somehow the storm's not mattering one bit to him. Not to me, either. We pick through all of the greens and find the freshest they have left. We search the shelves of the meat department for exactly the kind of bones my mother wants for her soup because she says the bones are what give it the flavor. And we buy lots of stuff she didn't even put on the list: root beer, black licorice, lupini beans, butterscotch pudding, hard salami. All the stuff he likes.

Funny how things are. How things turn out sometimes.

Root beer, black licorice, lupini beans, butterscotch pudding, hard salami. This is all the stuff I like, too.

PATIENCE. PATIENCE. PATIENCE.

"It still hurts, Ma." I say and lift the second spoon of Farina to my lips. It's sweet. It's milky. "Now it hurts on both sides and mostly when I swallow."

I'm not lying. It does hurt, but Farina is easy to get down. I don't listen to people who say it's food for babies. Who cares about the picture of the little baby on the box? I eat it anyway. Like Pastina. I eat that too.

I'm not a baby. No matter what everybody calls me, I'm still not a baby.

My mother stands on the metal, fold-up step stool and tries to find the flashlight.

"Just a minute, Kathy," she says. "Have patience, would you please?"

Patience. Patience. Patience.

"I'm going to take a look in that throat of yours just as soon as I find the goddamned flashlight!" She stretches up and stands on her toes. Her nightgown slides up and a big, purple vein bulges from the back of her leg, just under her knee. Gross.

The veins on her legs look like they hurt but she says they don't. They just look like they do. Roadmaps, she says. Roadmap legs. Maybe that's another reason I like the summer so much because in the summer her legs get real brown and she keeps her toes painted red or bright pink and it takes away from the roadmaps.

The stool rattles a little so I hop off of the kitchen chair and grab the metal edge and push it down hard into the floor. My fingers change color from how hard I push. I'm pushing hard on the stool because I can't even imagine what I would do if my mother fell off while she was looking for the flashlight. It would be all my fault. All because she needs to see if my tonsils are swollen and covered with pus.

She stretches back far and reaches her arm into the back of the cabinet.

"Got it?" I ask.

Even though I've thought about it maybe a million times I don't ask why we keep the flashlight all the way up there where it's so hard to reach. This is the kind of question I think about but don't ask. There are lots of questions like that, ones I think about but don't ask.

"Here it is." She pulls it out of the cabinet and slips it under arm. She steps off the stool carefully and once both of her feet touch the floor she says what she always says when she comes down from stools or ladders and even when she gets up out the recliner in our living room, the one she sits in most nights waiting for my brother's Camaro to pull up into our driveway and for his to come through the front door, usually in bad shape: "Oh, Jesus, Joseph and sweet Mother of God. Give me strength."

"Stay still and open wide, Love. C'mon, stay still!" She grabs my chin and pushes it down. I open my mouth real wide and think I might throw up because my breath stinks and tastes so bad. Sour, hot and heavy. It rolls right out of my mouth and into her face. Gross, again. If I were her right now, I'd be the one asking for strength.

"I see them. They're like clams, those tonsils of yours. And your breath. I can smell the fever."

How do you smell a fever? I close my mouth and lick my dry lips with my fever breath. "Why don't we have a thermometer like the Bentons?" I ask and sit back down at the kitchen table, back to my Farina. I remember when I had to bring Mary her homework every day after school because she was out sick for a whole week with croup. I walked into her house on one of those days and Mrs. Benton was standing over Mary's bed shaking her arm so fast I almost couldn't tell there was a thermometer in it. It was just a silver and red cloudy blur of a line. Even the charm holder that hung from the chain on Mrs. Benton's neck jingled. Once she stopped shaking I just stared at it. A thermometer. I wouldn't even know where to look for one in our house. My mother just smells our breath and presses her palm into our foreheads.

I finish almost all of the Farina and go to the bathroom. I pee and it burns probably because I used too much bubble bath last night.

My mother's voice swirls in my head: "One squirt of the bubble bath only! Did you hear me? Only one squirt!"

I go into my parents' bedroom and curl up on their bed. They have a soft, blue chenille bedspread and I wrap it around me. Their pillows smell like my father's cologne. He loves cologne and uses a lot of it. Sometimes when he gets all dressed up to go out with his buddies, his *paisans*, either to Atlantic City or to the Italian American club to play cards, my mother fixes his collar so it's straight in the back.

"Your father always smells so nice when he gets dressed up. Mother of God, they could smell that cologne in Canarsie for God's sake!"

These are the things my mother says when she straightens my father's collar.

WISE GUY

My mother is deciding on the beads she should to wear to work and I watch as she untangles them and lifts them off the porcelain statue of St. Jude that sits on the corner of her dresser. She keeps her necklaces and beads draped around the saints.

"Wear the yellow and blue one, Ma." I rub her Oil of Olay onto my elbows.

After she blames the sore throat on the fact that I didn't zip my jacket up all the way when I was riding my bike in the rain last weekend, we decide I'm sick enough to stay home from school. I am thrilled for three reasons. One, I will be alone for 5 hours, except for a few minutes here and there when Grandma Lucy will walk across the street (in between watching her stories) from her house to ours to check on me. She might bring me a glass dessert cup filled with red or green Jell-O. I'll eat it, she'll rinse the cup with water only (no dish soap, that's wasting) and she'll walk back home. Two, is that I'll be able to look at the dirty magazines my father keeps rolled up inside the newspapers next to the toilet in his bathroom. And three, because as long as I can figure out how to scoop the ice cream in a way that doesn't look like I ate a too much, I will have a big bowl of Breyers Vanilla for lunch and cover it with the green jimmies we use when we make Christmas cookies. The last time I stayed home by myself I did this and I used so many jimmies you couldn't even see one bit of vanilla in the bowl. Then when I went back to the couch to watch TV and rest I took a wet washcloth with me and scrubbed my lips hard. The green kind of blended in with the print on the washcloth since it had flowers all over it so, unless you were really looking for green jimmie stains, you'd never know a thing.

I can tell my mother feels bad about leaving me home alone so I tell her I am going back to my own bed, that I'm really tired.

"Good. Sleep is good," she says and blots her lipstick with a tissue. I love her lipstick. I love everything about it. She glances in the round mirror over her dresser, takes her two pointer fingers, licks them with her tongue and smooths down her eyebrows. It's a habit of hers that annoys my sisters but always makes me laugh.

I knew she wouldn't call in. She just started this job, as a bilingual aide at East Dover Elementary School. I love hearing about her days working with the kids who came from Italy to live with their families here on the Shore. I expected my father to make a mess about her getting a job and not doing the books up at the station anymore. But he didn't. My sisters said something about him not wanting her up at the station so much anymore anyway. About how he's in his own world up there. About his shenanigans.

A few nights ago, at dinner when she was talking about a girl named Pia, my father yelled out, "If they made the decision to come to America why the hell are they hiring you to speak Italian to them? They should speak English!" He chewed his bread hard with quick rough bites. Sometimes he ate so fast that he made these weird snorting sounds.

"Because they're children, Freddy. And they'll need a little help getting used to things here, that's why!"

"Yeah, yeah, yeah," my father moaned and sucked in hard on his cigarette. Just don't let me find out that principal of yours is giving you the eye." Then he pinched my cheek.

On that particular night, his mood was better than usual. Maybe that's why he pinched my cheek. He'd eaten three pieces of chicken cacciatore and even said it was pretty good, made just the way he liked it. So, she said, "What principal, Freddy? Don't be ridiculous!"

"C'mon, Catherine, don't bullshit a bullshitter! I know that Irishman has the hots for you! I saw the way he looked at you when I dropped you off at work. I'm no *stunad*." With the corner of his matchbook he picked at a piece of chicken caught in between his two front teeth. I got up from the table and went to the kitchen window, slipped two toothpicks from the little jar that we kept on the windowsill, handed one to him and kept one for myself.

I never met Mr. O'Malley. I guess he's Irish, like Mary.

One of the things my mother is really good at is knowing my father's moods. On that night when he was teasing her about the Irish principal she knew she could get away with being fresh back to him. When he asked her again if she sees the way the Irishman looks at her she laughed, smacked her hand on her hip so that we all heard a crack, kissed him on the forehead and said "Oh, Freddy, for God's sake don't be such a wise guy."

SHINY SUITS AND LEGS LIKE A ROCKETTE

There's this men's store named Braddock's where my father buys all his dress clothes. It's not far from our house, just a few miles down Route 37 heading toward the bridge to Seaside. Every few months he calls Gino, the guy who owns the place, to tell him he's coming. Braddock's isn't the only business Gino owns but I don't think he goes to Rotary Club meetings like my father so I'm really not so sure what kind of a businessman he is. According to my mother, Gino's all over the state of New Jersey, whatever that means. I'm not sure what he does but I guess it has to do with driving around because he's got two big shot cars. I think he goes up north a lot. Places like Bayonne, Newark, Elizabeth. Each December, I always see signs for these places when we take the New Jersey Turnpike to the Lincoln Tunnel to the Port Authority and then go see the Rockettes.

Like last year when we were driving in for the Radio City Music Hall Christmas Show. I was in the back seat but I heard my mother say to my sister, "Ria, slow down, for God's sake!" Then she told her to stop driving "like a bat outta hell." She let out a big breath and then said, "The last thing we need is a ticket."

She grabbed the edge of the dashboard and squeezed so hard her knuckles turned white. She's right. The last thing we do need is a ticket. Then my father will blast us. And then forget the Rockettes. Forget dinner at Patsy's. Forget lighting candles at St. Patrick's.

Ria just laughed and turned up her Bee Gees tape. "Doesn't that Gino guy, you know, the one who owns Braddock's, doesn't he know all the cops around here?" she asked my mother who was busy rubbing the inside bottom of her pocketbook, looking for quarters for the tolls.

My mother isn't the only one who wishes Ria would turn down the music. The Bee Gee brother with the real high voice makes me want to throw up. I saw a picture of them once on the cover of the album and decided I would never want a boyfriend with those big teeth and a high voice like that. I get grossed out just thinking about it.

"Don't we have one of those cards in the glove compartment?" Ria asked.

She was talking about the PBA card my father got from Gino. These are special cards you are supposed to show cops if you get pulled over. PBA stand for Police Benevolent Association and I only know that because I asked my mother once when they were talking about it. I guess the card tells them you know somebody, which seems pretty unfair to the people who don't.

"For crying out loud, you mean to tell me, you're not worried about getting pulled over because of the PBA card in the compartment?" My mother shook her head and made the clucking sound with her tongue that she makes when she's fed up with us. "You got a clear head," she said with a big, long sigh. "Just watch the road and take it slow." Then, a few shakes of the head. "Who wants his card anyway. That Gino's trouble!"

* * *

It's dinnertime. My father's plate is empty and clean. It always is. He wipes it clean with a piece of bread every single time he eats. His finished plate always looks like that, perfectly clean and smooth, no crumbs, no stains. You could just put it right back into the cabinet if you wanted to. Except that would be disgusting.

He gets up from the table, unbuttons his pants and burps really loud. He scratches his back on the wall next to the kitchen counter and then calls Gino to tell him he's ready come pick out some new clothes.

"I need new shirts, buddy, and not for nothing, Gino, but the pants you sold me six months ago, they're ripping all over the goddamned place!" He grabs a cigarette from the pack in his shirt pocket. I am picking at my rigatoni because I'm full, there's nothing else to do and *Good Times* doesn't go on for another hour. He looks at me and points to the lighter next to his dinner plate. I get up and grab it for him. It is heavy for a little silver lighter and cold, too. I love the way the top flips over and hangs down. It looks like it's going to fall off but it doesn't. I keep it closed and hand it to him.

I know better not to open it and even pretend like I'm lighting his cigarette. Once I did this, just as a joke, and he blew his top. I didn't even see it coming. He started screaming and my shoulders popped up close to my ears and my heart felt like it popped too, into my throat, even, because he just snapped and I got real freaked out. All I could do was stand there and try not to cry. My mother kept saying the usual.

"Ok, ok, that's enough now. Freddy, that's enough. She didn't mean anything by it." I closed my eyes, lowered my shoulders and tried to push my heart back where it belonged.

"I ain't raising my daughter to look like some tramp. Tramps light cigarettes like that!"

If, at that very moment, I had guts and a place to run away to I might have asked the question: How would you know?

It was just one of those nights. My mother says every house has them. Nights like that one. She says we never know what goes on behind closed doors so don't think we have it so bad here.

My father lights the cigarette, pinches me on the cheek and blows out a big cloud of smoke. "Good, all set," he says to Gino. "We'll see you next Monday and remember what I said about those frigging pants from last time!"

* * *

"Freddy, my boy," Gino says as we walk into his shop. He gives my mother a kiss and tells her he put Engelbert Humperdinck on just for her. He pinches my cheek and hands me a candy. Then Gino hugs my father and smacks him hard on his back. "You look good," he says. Gino is tall and skinny and his suit is very shiny. He smells like the whole cologne department at Bamberger's and there's a toothpick hanging out of his mouth that he keeps biting. "Freddy, I got some real nice new stuff to show you. Real nice. Sharp. Classy shit, Freddy, you'll see."

Braddock's is empty except for us. I walk to the back, go into the fitting room and check for feet under the doors. I'm alone so I sit on top of this small block. It's kind of a carpeted raised thing, like a little stage, and it's in front of three big mirrors. This part of the store reminds me of the movies. The ones with people who go to fancy stores, try on clothes and then get them taken in and out by little men and women with pins hanging out of their mouths. I sit down on this block, this little stage. I take my shoes off and cross my legs.

All I can do is look at myself in the three mirrors in front of me. I can't help it. I'm not used to so many mirrors, besides there's nothing else to do. Thank God there are no other customers out shopping tonight because it really grosses me out when we come here and men walk around in the fancy clothes they are thinking about buying and stare at themselves in the big mirrors. They pull on the silky ties and ask Gino if he has matching handkerchiefs. They button and unbutton

the jackets and ask their wives if they need a size bigger. They take out
their combs and slick their hair back as if the hair has anything to do
with the way the suit fits or if the buttons button.

We only have two mirrors in our house. One on the back of the door
to my parent's bedroom and one that's part of the medicine chest in the
bathroom. Because we never know what mood my father is in, I don't
use the one on their door very much which means that if I care about the
way I look from the neck down I have to stand on the ledge of the tub,
hold the shower curtain so I don't fall and look quickly at the medicine
chest mirror. And even then, I can only see up to my knees. When I do
this and my mother sees she makes the cracking sound and tells me to
get down because if I don't I'm going to fall and break my neck. When
I ask her if she really thinks I could break my neck by falling off the tub
ledge she tells me not to be fresh. "Don't be such a smart aleck."

I stand up and move from the front part of the shop fitting room
into an actual dressing room with a swing door. I look at myself again
in the mirror. I hate my legs. Everything about them. Their size, their
color. I wish I had Katie Horigan's legs. Long and skinny. Fair like the
French vanilla ice cream at Friendly's but not blotchy like Amy King's
face. Amy's skin is fair, too, probably the fairest in all of the sixth grade,
but it always gets red spots on it when we play kickball. Katie Horigan
has these little freckles on the front of her knees and the backs of her
knees have smooth, flat lines across them, not dimples like mine. I stared
at the back of Katie Horigan's legs in the locker room before gym the
other day and decided they were the legs I wanted if I could get new
ones. With legs like that, I bet if she really wanted to Katie Horigan
could be a Rockette someday.

We've been here about an hour already and Gino hasn't even started
talking price yet so I know it'll be a while. I finish the Tootsie Roll Gino
gave me and find one last piece of Big Red in the pocket of my jacket.
Now I'm just sitting here looking in the mirror trying to see how many
seconds I can hold it on my tongue before my eyes start to tear.

I walk out of the fitting room and see my father by the hat display
lighting a cigarette. Gino is in the front of the store on the phone arguing
with somebody about cuff links and my mother is by the sweater vests.
I start to walk to where my mother is but stop when my father says to
me, "Hey, Doll, c'mon over here."

He puts his cigarette in the ashtray on the counter, picks up a brown
wool cap and tries it on.

"Get a load of me in this one," he says and laughs. "I look like I just got off the boat!" His silly mood surprises me, I'm not used to it and it kind of comes out of nowhere. Reminds me of the day of the blizzard and what he looked like in the A&P. His eyes and the hat make him look like someone who tells the truth about everything.

I laugh and take a navy blue one off the rack for myself and slip it on over my braids. I may not have Rockette legs like Katie Horigan but my braids are very long and shiny. He winks at me, tugs my arm and pulls me over to the hat mirror. Sinatra's on the stereo now and my father is singing along to "The Best Is Yet to Come." We look at ourselves in the mirror. I wink back at him.

WHO DO YOU THINK YOU ARE?

My father sprinkles pepper onto his minestrone with angry shakes.

"He's like a frigging professor that guy! A big, goofy, professor."

He slurps his soup and goes on about Mr. Cunningham and how he wears flips flops and baseball hats. How he sits in his backyard and reads books.

This is a problem because the Cunningham house is right behind ours. It means we have no privacy. My father likes his privacy.

"Who the hell does he think he is?" he says with a glare.

"Freddy," my mother pleads. "Let it be, for God's sake. He's not hurting us."

"What the hell are you talking about! They're right on top of us!"

He pulls a cigarette from the pack in his front pocket and lights it with the Snap-On lighter he got from Dennis, the tool guy. Dennis gives stuff away all the time when he stops at Fred's Texaco. Mostly lighters and girlie calendars but once when I was there organizing the work orders and waiting for the phone to ring, he gave me a Charms pop.

"Where's my ashtray?" my father says and points to me. "You. Get up. Go get it for Daddy."

My mother pours him more soda because that's what she does when the glass gets to halfway. Every time, she pours more.

"I'm telling you Catherine, this guy thinks his shit don't stink. But that's over now. Today I talked to Frankie Jigs at Rodino Stone. Cement blocks are coming next week, on Tuesday so you better be here." She wipes the sweat from her neck with a dishtowel. He takes a gulp of his soda and announces, "I'm building a wall."

I find his ashtray in the living room on our new glass coffee table. It's the shape of a kidney bean and that's important because after the furniture company delivered it last month my mother told everyone about it. "It's a kidney shape. Very classy. It's what they're featuring now."

I hand my father the ashtray and sit back down to my soup and root beer. He pinches my cheek and says, "You gonna help me with this wall? I'll let you mix the cement."

I think about Mr. Cunningham and his family. His daughter, Caroline, is two grades ahead of me so she's not on my bus anymore. She's tall just like her dad. My mother says she looks like a Caroline. She doesn't say much, has red hair and wears tights in June which makes me itch just thinking about it. They're nothing like us. The whole family is tall and quiet. We're short and loud. But they seem alright to me. Not some crazy Peeping Tom family my father is making them out to be.

My mother asks him about whether we need to call the town about getting a permit and if we should tell the neighbors.

"That's bullshit! This is my house, my property. I'll build a wall if I want!" Then he mumbles again, something about Mr. Cunningham's books and feet and baseball hats. "Bet he's never fixed a frigging thing in his life."

"What's so bad about Mr. Cunningham?" I hear the last word leave my mouth and I panic. I want to shove every syllable back in. He looks my way. That glare. That glare means trouble. I feel bad. Like maybe now he won't want me to build the wall with him.

"Watch your tongue!" His small eyes are sharp and they cut into me. It's a bad paper cut times fifty.

"Who the hell do you think you are?" he says, eyes still slicing.

I put my head closer to my soup and slurp but the beans stop short right in front of my throat. My eyes water and my head burns. I can't answer but even if I could I wouldn't know how.

Who do I think I am?

He keeps barking, "Not for nothing, but chumps like him, they got no respect for guys like me. I don't need him looking at you."

He wipes the sweat from his sideburns with the napkin and tosses it into the pool of broth left in his bowl.

Time for another cigarette and another question: "Who the fuck does he think he is?"

We keep our traps shut. I take another spoonful of soup. It tastes like smoke so I have some bread and butter instead.

Who do I think I am?

RECESS

It's recess. I'm in the woods behind Cedar Grove Elementary School. Derek Brightman, bad boy of the sixth grade, sits next to a big oak tree and holds a black transistor radio in one hand and a crumpled picture from Playboy in another. I glance down at both but instantly shift my eyes up and away toward the tops of the trees. Some leaves are falling and some are not.

And then time stops for maybe a minute or two.

Before I run back to the tetherball game that I started playing earlier with George and Penny and Roger three things happen: First, I see Nancy Spelling and Johnny Fox in the distance, behind a honeysuckle bush, even farther back in the woods, kissing; Second, I hear "I want you to want me/ I need you to need me" blaring from Derek's radio; And third, something busts open inside of me and all of a sudden, I feel hungry.

But not for my lunch.

MAE MOON AND MARY GIRTAIN

It's Saturday afternoon at one o'clock and my mom and I are standing in Mae Moon trying to find the right-sized panties for Grandma Mac. Mae Moon is a store on Route 37 about ten minutes from the station and next to the Garden State Bank. We're running late, which always makes my mother nervous. And when she gets nervous, I get busy. I figure out plans for things. I figure out ways to get out or ways to get in. Or sometimes I just count whatever is around me. So now I'm counting panties and looking at myself in the big Mae Moon mirror.

The fact that Mae Moon wasn't in our original plan makes it even worse. The original plan was this: Garden State Bank to make the deposit for the station, Tice's Junkyard to pick up exhaust parts my father needs for two big jobs he's working on at the station, Charney's Stationary Store downtown to pick up rubber bands, a new stapler and masking tape, and, if there was time, Robert Hall, to look for my confirmation dress. Robert Hall is a store that sells clothes for the whole family. That's what the sign says. But only my mom, my sisters and I shop there. My father buys his dress clothes from Gino at Braddock's and I don't know where my brother, Jack, gets his clothes. When he's not wearing his station uniform (the same one my father wears: grey Dickies and light grey shirts with their names embroidered in red on over the pocket on the right) Jack wears the exact same thing over and over: beige corduroy Levis and a red and black flannel shirt. Maybe my mother buys his clothes at Grants or it wouldn't surprise me one bit if he just wears stuff he finds lying around at his troublemaker friends' houses.

But the plan fell apart. We made the deposit and then we landed here. At Mae Moon.

"We're right here, for God's sake," she said as we walked out of the bank. That was about twenty minutes ago. I could tell she wanted to add a stop to our plan. I could just tell by the way she was shaking her head, glancing at her watch and pointing to the store. "I'll be ten minutes, at the most. I know exactly what I need. Grams likes the styles they sell here."

"So, let's go then," I said.

"Alright, we'll make it quick. In and out. No killing time. Who the hell wants to hear his mouth if we're late? And don't say nothing about Mae Moon. The shit will hit the fan if he knows I'm buying for her."

This is one of those times when I say nothing to my mother because all the things I would say at this moment would make her feel bad about the whole situation. About her not being able to see her own mother, my Grandma Mac. The only real reason ever given to me about why she can't see her mother goes like this: "Your father can be as good as gold sometimes but when it comes to this he's a son of a bitch bastard."

That's all I know.

My mother hates thinking too much about the crosses she has to bear, whatever that means, and she also hates what she calls killing time. Dilly-dallying. I think that she thinks if we move fast through Mae Moon and get the panties quick it won't hurt so much when she remembers that she's not even allowed to bring them to her own mother. Then what will probably happen after she buys my Grandma Mac's panties will make no sense at all.

But making sense isn't high on the list around here. She'll lie to my father and he'll never know about the panties. That's if we're lucky. She might even write a check for the next batch of groceries that's more than what the groceries cost. She does that sometimes and Charlie, the manager at A&P, lets her. She writes the check for a little more than the price of the groceries and then this way she'll get some money back. But when my father sees the checkbook he'll think it's all for groceries.

It's not that my father is a stingy man. He's not. Sometimes he's the opposite of stingy. Like when he's in a good mood and I'm going to the movies with Mary and Kim, he'll just hand us a twenty and say, "Tell you what I'm gonna do. Popcorn and candy, on me!"

He's not stingy but if things aren't going his way and he's crooked, he can be pretty mean. He's mean mostly when it comes to Jack smoking the shit he smokes, my mother wanting to see her family and my sister, Lucy, wanting what I think seems like just a pretty good life to me—going to college, getting married and becoming a teacher. Apparently, these things, and probably a whole list of other stuff, don't sit well with him and so sometimes he blows up.

The good moods, the popcorn-and-candy-on-me-days are unusual lately and it seems like my mother lies about everything that has to do with Grandma Mac, the rest of her family, my brother and Lucy. My father never uses anyone's name when it comes to my mother's relatives, he just says Them. So now, when it comes to Them he says he's finished and she better not push it. And when he gets wound up about it he tells my mother what she can and can't do. Or else they'll be trouble.

Or he throws stuff.

So, she's still not allowed to see them. She still sneaks visits. And I help her.

* * *

I've counted thirty-two panties so far. The deposit slip from the bank is sticking out of the pocket of my jeans. I see it when I look at myself in the big Mae Moon mirror. It's my job to hold on to the deposit slip and give it to my father when we get back to the station after our errands, what my mother calls, our stops. I used to love this job when I was little, but now that I'm twelve it's just a big pain. I can even remember a time when we'd pull back into the station, after our stops, and my father would smile and look real happy to see us. Especially my mother. He'd smack her on her ass and say, "What took you so long, Doll?" And she'd smile. Maybe I'd even dance and sing for all the customers in the Waiting Room. No shows these days.

The mirror on the Mae Moon wall is between the big rack of panties and the counter with all the boxes of stockings stacked inside. Sometimes we get Grandma Lucy her stockings here, too and, when we do, the sales lady has a special way of opening the shiny boxes and pulling out the silky, tan nylons. It's cool to watch because she acts like the stockings are precious jewels or something else very, very valuable. And I guess they are to the people who wear them. I've seen the way Grandma Lucy washes them in the bathroom sink and then hangs them on the shower rod. They are special. Except for the fine, warm hair on the inside of my dog Lady's stomach these nylons are the softest things I've ever touched that's not on a person. The skin on the inside of the top of my mother's arms is probably the softest people thing I've touched.

Or maybe the inside of Kevin Schmidtt's arm which I got to touch last week when we were doing tug of war in gym. But he likes Nancy Jacobs so I don't even want to think about that now.

My two grandmas are the only people I know who wear these stockings. They only go up to the middle of the thighs then they hook onto a girdle with these funny white straps that have rubbery clips on the end. The fancier version of this is at Frederick's but my mother calls that store a whole a different ball game. Mae Moon is an old lady store. A store for grandma clothes, in mostly big sizes and what my people call bloomers and under things. Girdles and dusters, too. Fredericks is a floozy store and I doubt anybody calls the things they sell bloomers.

Seeing the deposit slip hang there out of my pocket makes my tongue quiver and collect water. It reminds me of the bank again. In the green leather bank deposit bag we use to deliver the money there's a lemon lollipop. Put there by Mrs. Mary Girtain, Head Teller. And it's mine. Mrs. Girtain knows me by now, because of all the deposits we make, and she never forgets to give me a lollipop. I thought when I turned twelve, she might stop, but she didn't. She's a nice lady who always wears animal pins on the collars of her blouses. I can't say for sure but I'd bet she buys her bloomers at Mae Moon, too. Every time we get into the car after we see her at the bank my mother says the same thing, "She's a sweetheart that Mary Girtain but she's had a tough life. I can tell."

HALF BRITISH, HALF RICH PEOPLE

We are finishing our Saturday morning housecleaning when my father calls. I'm kneeling on the floor, next to the coffee table in the living room picking up the pistachio shells my brother left there from when he was watching TV last night. Probably *Starsky and Hutch* or *The Streets of San Francisco*. One of those stupid cop shows. He's such a jerk sometimes, my brother. He thinks all I am good for is cleaning up his messes and covering for him.

I'm daydreaming and wishing I lived somewhere else. Nantucket like the girl in the book I'm reading or maybe Florida, by Disney World. Maybe even Italy! Anywhere but here. I'm really far away because the sound of the phone makes me jump.

"Put your mother on the phone, I need her to pick up a part at Chevy," my father says in his hoarse and raspy voice. It's from smoking, I know it, because everyone who smokes has that same voice. And another thing, my father never says hello or goodbye on the phone. I bet he thinks doesn't need to waste his breath on hellos and goodbyes.

My mother is cleaning the front hall mirror with a rag that is drenched in vinegar and water. I smell it from here. I like Pine Sol and Pledge better. They might be strong but at least they don't make everything smell like an *antipasto* or like the juice in the jars of shriveled peppers my mother puts on salad.

"Ma, telephone!"

She walks over to grab the phone. She looks so tired. Her hair is wrapped in a floral, yellow and turquoise satin scarf that she sometimes ties around the handle of her pocketbook.

"Nothing wrong with a little color once in a while," she said the night she bought it at Grant's Department Store. She pulled the tags off of it and tied it to the handle before we got out of the car and walked inside the house. That was about a year ago. She didn't want my father to see everything we bought at Grant's because, as she said and still says whenever we go to Grant's, "Who the hell wants to hear his mouth?" So, we did that sometimes. If we bought stuff and we didn't want to hear his mouth we'd take the tags off and wear it inside or just wait until he was out or at work to bring the bags in. Another trick of hers, I guess. Like Charlie and the checkbook.

She's got an old apron on over her blue and white striped shirt with the three-quarter sleeves. Now it's got a tear and a bleach stain by the neck but I remember when she bought that, too.

She laughed when I told her it looked like a shirt somebody would wear on a big fancy sailboat. But it did. She said it was because of the stripes and the sleeves. "Jackie O style," she mumbled with an accent that sounded half British, half rich people. She looked beautiful the first time she wore it. It was last summer, in July, when we all went to the boardwalk together. I remember that night and couldn't forget it for a second even if I tried. My father never usually came with us when we went out for fun but that night he did. Most of the time, he went his way and we went ours. At least that's the way my mother put it when I asked why he goes down to Atlantic City so much all by himself. But that night on the boardwalk, my mother in her new striped tee shirt with the three-quarter sleeves, her skin tan and the pink lipstick she's been wearing forever but always makes her look new, and my father buying us bags of red and black licorice and wearing the light green shorts we bought him on sale. It all looked so perfect. It all was so perfect. Who could forget a night like that?

"Who is it?" she whispers as if the person on the other end is a big secret.

"It's Daddy and why are you whispering?" I say in a whisper back. I know I'm being a smart aleck but I don't care. I hate this Saturday cleaning, I hate that scarf on her head and I hate that she's going to have to stop everything and run to bring things to my father and the guys at the station. And she's going to want me to tag along. I just know it.

She tells me "Watch it!" and wipes the top of her lip with the rag of dust and vinegar.

I go back to the pistachio shells.

WANTING WHAT'S AT PINEVIEW CHEVY

"I knew it. I knew we'd get stuck here!" I mumble in a tone that is beyond crooked to my mother as we walk from the back office of the gas station to the car. We've been here almost an hour already after getting the call to stop what we were doing, go to Pineview Chevy, pick up the fan belt the Parts Manager was holding for Fred's Texaco and deliver it up to the station. "And don't dilly dally," I bet my father said to her when he called with his orders, "I got customers waiting here and I'm busting my ass."

It wasn't so bad coming to Pineview Chevy for parts because they have good candy machines in the customer waiting room. They've got M & M's, packs of Juicy Fruit and lemon jawbreakers.

Candy again. I love unexpected, always-filled-and-never-missing-anything vending machines. I still love that Mary Girtain, the bank lady, and Dennis, the tool guy, give me candy. It make things easier sometimes.

But most of all, and maybe even more important than candy right now, Pineview Chevy is not so bad because the guy who works behind the counter is so cute I can't even believe it. Surfer-type, so I have no idea why he's working the parts desk at Chevy but he's still so nice to look at. He makes things a little easier too.

Blue eyes, curly blond hair. Different. In a good way. He reminds me of Valerie Luddington's brother. Valerie is in the seventh grade with me and my mother hates when I ask if I can go to her house after school. She lives across town in a development called Penny Lane or Penny Crossing or something like that. Valerie's mother has long blond hair and long blond legs. "They go on forever, those legs of hers," my mother says, but not in a way that seems like a compliment.

Also, according to my mother, Valerie's mother stays home all day and does crafts. The last time I was invited there to hang out, we pulled up to her house and there was a big wooden, handmade sign with flowers and raccoons painted on it. In the middle of the wood, in perfectly shaped yellow letters were two words: Welcome Friends.

I leaned over to give my mother a kiss goodbye and she mumbled, "What the hell is that for? She's a got clear head that Valerie's mother.

Who has time to make do-dads like that?"

Personally, I don't know what Valerie's mother does all day long. But I do know that their house always smells like warm cookies, her brother's cute and they go camping. This is what I mean about liking stuff that's different.

Earlier while my mother was looking for a parking space in the Chevy lot, I grabbed a few quarters from the coin holder in the console and dabbed on a little of her lipstick before we came inside. I tried not to want the candy and the boy with the blue eyes every single time we had to pick up a fan belt or a set of brake pads or an oil filter. But it's hard when you try to not want something. You want it even more. And if it's different than what you are used to or what you should be wanting, then you're in big trouble.

WAITING BY WINDOWS II

"Where the hell is he?" my mother asks the nobody she always asks when this happens. "I could choke that brother of yours sometimes!"

I am behind her, running my pinky finger along the soft brown stripe of velour on her robe. She got it for Christmas last year from my sisters and after she unwrapped it and opened the box they all called it champagne but it's just tan to me with a few brown stripes by the zipper and down the back in the middle. Anyway, I'm saying a Hail Mary that my father doesn't get out of the shower before my brother pulls up after being out all night, gallivanting. Gallivanting. That's what my mother says. It's more than just gallivanting, though.

It's pot. It's speed. It's probably lots of other stuff, too.

Hopefully, if this morning goes like all the others, my brother will park on the street, a few doors down, by the Wilsons. And hopefully my father will still be in the shower or gluing his hairpiece on his head or shaving. If things go right, my brother will grab his work uniform from my mother. She'll be holding it on a hanger with one arm out the door and still shaking her head but with eyes that shut every few seconds, too, like she can't bear to look anymore. I can tell even looking at him with his eyes all bloodshot and his cheeks bony and covered with pimples, it makes her want to just fall down and go to sleep. Want to just start all over. I feel like that sometimes.

Does she? Does he?

But she'd never do that. She'll just say to the nobody again, "I'm so disgusted." Then she'll whisper, the same words, shake her head in the same way, like always, and close her eyes every few seconds. She will have already checked that it's the right uniform. She's done this so many times before, waited by the window for him to come home.

After he sees her there waiting, he'll walk up to the door, look at her face through the window of the metal door, grab the hanger and say, "Thanks, Ma." She'll throw him a pack of Sen Sen and tell him his breath smells like shit and that he better straighten himself out.

But, for now, she's still waiting at the front door looking out the window.

And I'm behind her.

NERVES

I know my mother, father and I all see the big sign that says Carrier Clinic.

"This is it," my mother says looking down at the little slip of paper she's holding that has notes on it in her handwriting. "And make the next right. The counselor on the phone said the Visitor Lot is the first right."

My father says nothing. From the backseat of our Lincoln I can see his cigarette ash is very, very long and I think it's going to fall any minute now. His face is puffy and he has little pieces of tissue stuck to his neck in all the places he cut himself shaving.

I'm sweating and have the chills at the same time. I woke up like this.

My mother says it's nerves because she felt my forehead when I sat at the kitchen table eating my cereal. "You're fine. You're not warm at all," she mumbled. "Go get dressed."

So, I guess she's right. Nerves.

My brother meets us in the lobby of what everyone is calling the place Jack needed to go for a while to straighten himself out.

Carrier has an excellent reputation. Carrier has helped so many people. Carrier has a bed. Carrier this. Carrier that.

This is what I told Mary the other day after the huge fight about how short the shift was at the station, about the shit my father found in Jack's car, about how my father thought for sure he'd knock the sense into him and, as my mother kept saying when my brother banged the inside door of his room wanting to get out, that dope shit out of him by keeping him locked in his room for five days: "I'm really, really scared."

"I'll detox him," my father said.

That didn't work and I knew it for sure when I heard my mother say in between the screams and noises from fists (both my father's and Jack's) banging on the walls, "He needs help, Freddy. Can't you see what this shit is doing to him. He's like a mess in that room. My poor son, that shit is making him into an animal."

So now here we are. In the lobby of Carrier Clinic. The place that straightens people out.

RED, BROWN AND NAVY BLUE

Jack's scabs are back. Crusty and mostly brown but there are some red ones, too, and they go up and down his skinny arms. On the top of his arms he used to have smooth, round muscles that looked like baseballs when he flexed which always made my mother say, "Sure, this one's Hercules with those arms."

Carrier didn't work.

I told him once he had Popeye the Sailor Man arms. Except Popeye lost his baseballs again and now it's just skin and scabs. Some of the scabs are round like mosquito bites but there are a few rectangular ones, too. I spend tons of time looking at my brother's arms.

One of them even looks like the bad scrape I got on the back of my ankle last Tuesday when the screen door closed too fast and I lost my balance. I was wearing my new, navy blue Dr. Scholl's and still wasn't used to the bump under my toes. The special bump that's supposed to make legs skinnier. That's what the ad says.

"You're going to break your neck in those things," my mother snapped when we were in Grant's two weeks ago and I waved the pair of the sandals I wanted in front of her. "Ma, please," I begged. She caved fast but, when I think about it now, I'm not surprised. These days she's exhausted and worried more than ever before and I know this because she always tells me, "No one knows what I got inside the pit of my stomach. I'm sick over all this."

So, things are back to being all mixed up and a mess. So, she didn't actually say yes to the Dr. Scholl's but just motioned to put the shoebox in our shopping cart. Then she sighed that famous long, hard sigh. She was fed up, I could tell. "Alright, let's go pay," she said and pushed the cart toward the registers. When we stopped to wait next to the other shoppers who were buying summer shoes and bathing suits I noticed the white eye shadow she put on that morning looked grey now and there was a loose bobby pin just above her ear sticking up and coming out of her beehive hairdo. Jim would be real upset if he saw her right now.

While we waited together to pay the Grant's cashier something hit me: I realized that she wasn't the only one who was fed up. I was, too, but with myself. I was about to take the box back to the shoe department and say, Ma, I changed my mind. but then the cashier said "Next!" so I just put them on the counter with our other stuff, new panties and the stockings she was buying for the lady on our block who doesn't leave her house.

My mother is always bringing things to people.

The truth of it all is this: I got the shoes because Jack's using again. My mother has had it up to here. She walks around with bobby pins falling out of her hair and dirty-looking eyelids. She's tired, scared and worried and I should have just kept my trap shut about the sandals.

Navy blue Dr. Scholl's that can make fat legs skinny are the last thing she should be thinking about.

* * *

"Jack, stop picking at that," I say. "It's so gross."

It's eight o'clock on a Wednesday night and we're lying on the couch in our den, eating pistachio nuts and watching *The Waltons*. He stops picking at his arm and then he starts throwing his empty shells, one by one, into the ashtray on the coffee table. When he does this, I notice the scabs even more because he's moving his arms around.

My mother's lectures the last couple of years, the ones about Jack getting clean and staying clean obviously didn't work. Then Carrier didn't work either. It's not just Baggies of reefer and clips with feathers on the ends that he hides in stupid places like his underwear drawer and the console of his Camaro. It's not just little copper bottles with white powder inside.

There are needles now.

He calls it crank but my mother still calls it shit. I only know what they call it and where he hides it because I snoop. I spend almost as much time snooping as I do looking at my brother's arms.

Which brings me back here, to the den. I zero in on his arms again when he throws the nutshells. I try not to dwell because my mother is always telling me, "Don't dwell, for God's sake!"

I pray instead. God, help him stop. God, straighten him out. God, clean him up.

Then I wonder if I should be saying make him stop instead of help him stop.

Can God make somebody stop?

"Ha, ha," I tease when he misses the ashtray. Then I smile which is screwed up and weird. What do I think? That we have a white picket fence in our front yard and sit around and eat apple pie all the time.

This worries me. Why am I teasing and smiling with Jack like everything's okay?

We're not a white-picket-fence-apple-pie family.

We're not the Waltons.

He laughs a small laugh and I wonder if he's high. These days, I'm always wondering if he's high, staying up all night and what I remember somebody at Carrier saying: strung out. Then he tosses a whole nut at me and laughs again. I smile again. This is both weird and nice at the same time.

But I don't throw any back at him. I want to but I don't. I can't. I want us to be like the brothers and sisters on television, like the families on television, who play football in their front yards on Thanksgiving and toss nutshells at each other for fun. But we're not like that. So, I let him toss the shells at me and I don't toss any back.

We finish watching *The Waltons* and he says, "I'm outta here." Then he grabs the keys to his Camaro and screeches out of the driveway. I slip my feet into my new Dr. Scholl's. I want to ask God for skinny legs but decide to hold off until Jack gets clean. So, I take a walk around our block three times instead.

PLAYING CHECKERS WITH RICHIE

My father is a son of a bitch bastard. That's what my mother calls him sometimes and I agree although I might add fascist, bastard and dickhead to the list. Even Grandma Lucy, his own mother, has her own litany about it: "He'll never change, my Freddy. Stubborn like a bull, that one! A real *capa tosta*. I got one son without a pot to piss in and one that can't keep his trap shut." The one without the pot is my Uncle Anthony who my father says never has a nickel in his pocket and who lives down on Route 37 in a small apartment right before the bridge and next to Stew's Bait and Tackle Shop. I've been to Stew's. You'd think the place would smell like fish. It doesn't. It smells like cat pee and garlic.

Enough about Uncle Anthony except that he goes to the dog track all the time and that he has a wife, my Aunt DeeDee, and two kids, Janice, who's fourteen and Dominic, who's almost twenty. I know a lot about them, and that's another story, but all that matters to me these days is that they both like Alice Cooper, python snakes and black nail polish. My mother feels bad for them and the way they live, so sometimes she brings things to them, too. Macaroni, cans of crushed tomatoes, milk, toilet paper, juice, eggs.

* * *

Even though I have a long list of crappy names I call my father, last week when we were at Connie and Salvatore's house for coffee and cake something really weird happened that made me think again about it. The list, I mean.

Salvatore and my father both go to the Italian American club and Connie knows my mom from the beauty parlor, so they are all good friends. Kind of like how Dotty and Dave were with them when we lived in Ship Bottom. I think Connie's real name is Constantina but nobody ever calls her that. They own a butcher shop on Clinton Boulevard and that's where my mother buys most of her meat except cold cuts. She gets those at the A&P. Once I asked her why we don't get everything at Salvatore and Connie's store and she said, "Connie and Salvatore are as good as gold, but I can't be running all over God's creation for a half a pound of ham."

We were at their house to celebrate Richie's 21st birthday. Richie is Connie and Salvatore's son and he's slow. My cousin, Joanie, once asked my mom what's up with Richie and even though I was in the den watching television I listened in and heard her say something about an accident when he was a little boy and I could have sworn she said it had to do with a shopping cart in a parking lot. It all made me so nervous and scared and I kept thinking about Richie's face, his arm that always moved by itself, his funny smile, about how the spit runs down one side of his mouth, and how his teeth never seem like they are brushed. Right then and there I promised myself that every time I go to the A&P or to Acme with my mom I'd bring the cart back up to the front of the store. And that's what I do now. Whenever I am at a grocery store I make sure I slip the cart back into the long row of carts and before I let go all the way I make sure it is in, nice and tight.

After we sang Happy Birthday that night I saw my father take Richie by the arm and walk him from the kitchen into the family room. My mother and Connie were clearing the table and I was supposed to be helping them but after a few minutes I couldn't help walking away from the dirty plates and coffee cups when I heard Richie's loud laughs coming from the other room. I peeked in and almost died! Salvatore was in his leather recliner watching the news and smoking a cigar and my father and Richie were playing a game of checkers. Checkers. I've never seen my father touch a checker or play a game.

"Richie, what do you say, buddy. You're a man now, wanna smoke?" My father pinched Richie's cheek, offered him a cigarette, reached over and smacked him on the shoulder the way he does when the Pontoriero cousins from up north come to visit. It all looked so buddy, buddy. And Richie? He was laughing and shaking and smacking my father back on his shoulder, too. He pushed the cigarette away and said, "Freddy, you're crazy, Freddy. Freddy, you're crazy. Crazy Freddy. Crazy Freddy!"

Salvatore was laughing, too, and he said, "Hey Richie, maybe Freddy will give you a job one day up at the station?"

My father sucked in hard on his cigarette and flicked his ash into the ashtray on the side table. "Richie, your turn, big man." He looked at Salvatore. "You bet. You want to come work on cars, Richie? I'll teach you. What kind of cars do you like, buddy?"

Richie moved his piece and called my father crazy again but kept right on smiling and laughing.

I thought about how when I am with Richie I get all nervous and worried about what I will say and how I am supposed to act. I think lots of people get this way around him. But there I was looking at Richie and my father playing checkers and acting like it was the easiest thing in the world to be doing. Richie was loving it, I could tell from the look on his face. And my father was, too. His mean eyes were different that day in Connie and Salvatore's family room.

I got back to the table in time to clear the milk pitcher and the sugar bowl. It looked like the special china, shiny white glass with silver and yellow flowers, so I carried them carefully to their china cabinet in the corner of the kitchen.

"Mrs. DiSavio, should I put these in here?" I asked.

"Yes, dear, that's right. Just put them right back in there."

I put the milk pitcher down on the countertop, just for a minute while I opened the glass door. My hand was shaking because I knew this was the good stuff, the good china, all put out for Richie's birthday. We took the good stuff out at our house, too, on special occasions. But special didn't always mean happy. Once the good china platter, filled to the top with rigatoni and meatballs, got smashed right into the side wall of our dining room. It knocked the picture of us in the Bahamas, me with my Better in the Bahamas tee shirt and my mother in her big straw hat, right down to the floor. All because my brother walked in twenty minutes late smelling like weed.

So, in the most careful way ever, I placed the milk pitcher and the sugar bowl back in Connie and Salvatore's china cabinet and made sure they were pushed away from the edge and all the way in, nice and tight.

HEALTH

I'm in Health and bored out of my fucking mind. We're learning about the four food groups which seems like such a joke because nobody I know wakes up in the morning and is in the mood for half a grapefruit, two scrambled eggs, whole wheat toast and a cup of coffee. Mr. Dean just taped a big poster on the board in the shape of a pyramid. Now he's separating the pyramid into four parts with his big, fat Magic Marker that smells so good. He labels each part: Protein. Dairy. Fruits/Vegetables. Grains.

"I love the smell of Magic Markers," Johnny Katavalos whispers to me.

"Me too," I say.

Johnny sits in front of me in Health, Spanish and Home Ec. He's got green eyes, curly black hair and really big ears but his hair is kind of long most of the time so you only notice the ears when he gets a haircut. Tara Stittle says he likes me but I think she's just saying that to get something started. She's always starting stuff for no reason. I could like him if I thought about it. He's kind of cute, I guess. But not as cute as Maurice Evans who sits in the back two rows behind me. I never told anybody I think Maurice is cute, though.

Johnny's family owns the diner down on Elm Street and he works there on the weekends. I saw him last month when my mom and I went for breakfast after church and he had on a white shirt, black pants and a black bow tie. He looked very professional except for the big, square grey bucket with dirty cups and saucers inside that he was lugging around with him.

"Hey," he said to me when he passed our table. He had a big ketchup stain on the back of his shirt.

"Hey," I said back.

"Who's the Greek?" my mother said when he walked away.

"Shhhhh," I said in a hush. I hate when I don't know if something is wrong or right, like calling someone a Greek.

Mr. Dean tells us that everybody needs to choose one of the food pictures he has on the front table. He tells us this is an exercise and that once we choose our picture it will be our job to sit back in our seats, think about what it is a picture of and what group it fits into. Then, one by one, we will tell the class our answers and tape the pictures onto the pyramid in the right spot. This is the dumbest thing I ever heard of. I feel like a three-year-old.

He points to the first row of desks in the room. "Row One. Up. Get up and get your food pictures." He signals to us by pointing and clapping his hands. "C'mon, now. No horsing around! You people are young adults. Act like it!"

Someone in the back fakes a sneeze and "fuck you" is heard in between the ahchoo. Mr. Dean glares at the back row of kids and says, "Watch it, Mister" to Brian Dennegin who Tara says smokes pot on the weekend with his older brother in the woods over by Windsor Avenue. I wonder if that's where my brother used to go before he moved up in the world of what my mother still calls shit. Before speed. Before needles.

Row One goes then he points to Row Two, claps, they go, then Row Three, another clap and then Four, the row that me, Maurice, Johnny and this girl named Amy Littleton are in. Maurice says he needs to go to the Boy's Room so he takes the pass and leaves the classroom. By the time the rest of us in Row Four get to the front table there are only three pictures left: a bowl of soup, a nut and a steak. Johnny takes the steak and I take the nut because I listened to the directions and I know Mr. Dean expects answers. I always listen to the directions even when I try not to. I don't know if the soup is a protein or a vegetable so that's why I take the nut. Amy is left with the soup which makes me feel a little bad because she has pimples all over her face and she itches her elbows all the time so everyone makes fun of her. She's probably the last person who needs to deal with the picture of the soup bowl.

I think about Maurice and wonder when he'll be back and if he will want to share my picture. I think about his smooth, beautiful brown skin and long eyelashes. One time I stared at his eyelashes for a whole class period.

I think about Johnny and his green eyes and thick dark hair. I think about Pineview Chevy guy. His blond curls and blue, blue eyes.

"Kathy, hold up your picture and tell us what it is," Mr. Asshole Dean barks.

I try to shake Johnny's eyes and surfer boy's curls out of my head. I hold up the picture and say, "I got a nut."

"And?" Dean presses.

Maurice walks back into the room.

"Mr. Evans please turn your attention to Kathy. She has the floor."

I hate him and this whole dumbass lesson.

"And I guess it could be both a protein and a fruit," I say and glance at Maurice who is walking toward me.

Before Asshole Dean could say anything else I add, "I mean because they give you energy and grow on trees, right?"

I hate my answer.

"Wrong!" Dean barks again but I don't hear anything else he says because Maurice comes up right next to me, sort of even leans into me and reaches out for the card. His beautiful, brown fingers touch mine.

It's different, times one thousand.

PINKY RINGS AND ROASTED PEPPERS

My father's diamond and gold pinky ring is all I can see even though my eyes are slammed shut and Mike Donato is pushing his slimy tongue into my mouth.

In between the tongue pushing he says, "Jesus, you're so hot. Your skin is so soft." His breath smells like beer and Doritos and his neck like Aramis. Then more ridiculousness, "I want you tonight," he says. "I want you so bad."

My back is jammed up against the handle of the hall locker. We are way down on the other end of the school by the cafeteria, far from the gym where the dance is. We are where we're not supposed to be which is new for me but I'm a freshman in high school now so everybody says I should get with it. I mean in terms of with guys and stuff. I slip my hands into Mike's back pockets because I love back pockets. Not all back pockets, just certain ones. Maybe it might get me into the mood of all this.

But it doesn't work. Not this time. Not this guy. Not these pockets. Instead I feel my stomach turn.

"Mike, um, hold on a sec. Slow down."

I pull my face back from his and notice the sweat on his temples. He takes my hand and moves it to the zipper of his pants. Big mistake. When I first saw him tonight, he was walking from his silver Mustang to the door of the school where we had agreed to meet, his pants were the thing I noticed immediately. They annoyed me the minute I saw them. They were silly looking dress pants. They were black and shiny and way too tapered at the ankle. They were what my mother might call atrocious.

The black pants are what got me to thinking about my father's pinky ring. And that, mixed with the Dorito breath and the stupid comments, ruined everything.

* * *

"Volkswagens are a pain in the ass to fix, do you hear me? What the hell do you want with some beat up VW anyway?"

We're at the dinner table and my father is reading the newspaper, putting out his cigarette, cutting his veal with the side of his fork and blasting me all at the same time.

"That's not what Stacy Budney and her parents say. They all have bugs!" I move the red roasted peppers around on my plate and decide not to eat them tonight. They make me burp too much and I always feel like I am eating them all over again.

My father looks up from the paper and glares. "I've been busting my ass all my life, trying to build a business. Fixing cars. Pumping gas. All my life, for God's sake."

I toss my napkin onto my plate and start to get up from the table. Here we go. Just like the peppers. All over again.

"Sit your ass back down, damn you. I'm not finished!"

Finished? I could've told him he wasn't finished. I could have told him that. Nobody around here is ever finished, because nothing ever ends. Not the fights, not the lies, not the worries, not the tears. I do as he says. I sit my ass back down. And when I do I think about this nothing-ever-ending-all-over-again nightmare of a life. And when I find myself wondering if I will run from it all someday I hear him mumbling about some schoolteachers named Budney who drive shitwagon cars. About how he works hard like a dog and how people talk down to him.

My mother starts rearranging the serving dishes. She moves the cutlets where the salad was and the salad where the breadbasket used to be. The basket of bread she moves to the end of the table and throws a dirty *moppina* on top of it. It tips over and crumbs spill out. That's another thing that never ends: her tolerance for him.

"C'mon Freddy, don't start."

He pushes his plate away and slips another cigarette from the pack. The matchbook is empty so he gets up and uses the stove. "This is the thanks I get. My daughter wants to drive around in some beat up piece of shit. For what?" Now he's shaking his head, too. "So people can say her father can't rub two nickels together?" He's on a roll. I've seen it before. "I take care of my family. I can do that without some fucking degree and big fucking office."

I space out because of the lunacy of it all. Who said anything about offices and degrees? He goes on to say something about not being allowed to have a Volkswagen because then what do you do when you have to pay your respects at a funeral? Or a wake? Or some affair? I hate when my parents call parties affairs. All I can think is this: The only affair I know anything about is the one you're having with that bitch named Sally.

My mother shoots me her look. I am to keep my mouth shut. And I do.

The gold chain on his neck is caught on some of the curly, gray hair on his chest. It's just a matter of time before he will turn a certain way and it will pull and pinch his skin. I want to untangle it but I wouldn't even know where to start.

PRESSING PLAY

I'm in Deer Hollow Park, the playground where little kids don't play anymore and, according to my mother, troublemakers go. "When Doves Cry" is on my new Walkman and I'm spooked because I've already played it seven times over and over and am now pressing Play for the eighth time which makes me think that I might be going crazy.

I'm sitting on a black rubber swing, swaying. It's just before dark. No one else is here in the park and I pray to the Gods of the Confused Hungry Teenage Souls that someone is watching me.

How is it that I want to be all alone, but, at the same time looked at, glanced over and watched? I don't know how that happens, but I know I want both.

Prince's smooth voice moves through me. Then up, in, out and around.

I regret sharpening, burning and applying the brown eyeliner to both the inside and outside of my eyelids this morning when I put on my makeup. I should've used black.

There's a huge difference between the brown and black and even though I wasn't ready for the black this morning, I'm ready now.

BARMAID

Sally is everything my mother is not. Tall and skinny. A fake redhead. A smoker and a barmaid (What is a barmaid anyway and why is it a word?). And Sally's also the wearer of either long, flowing polyester pants with very high, wide waistbands or short, straight skirts with zippers up the back. It's for these reasons and lots more that make her nothing like my mother.

I could go on and on.

I don't remember the first time I saw her. Why would I? For a long time, she was just another customer, another brake job, another new alternator, another gas tank needing a fill up. Probably in those days, the days when she first started coming around, I was too worried about Jack and all his shit—what he's smoking, snorting and shooting up— to notice that Sally was way more than just another regular customer at Fred's Texaco. No actually, she was and still is way more.

But now I know. She's a regular all right. A regular bitchwhorefloozytramp who drives a white Mark V with maroon interior, who works the day shift at the Miracle Lounge and chews Dentyne, as my mother might say, a mile a minute.

THE STATEMENTS

I'm at work. Again. It's Saturday all over again. Most kids I know love Saturdays. I hate them. Saturday means up early and spending the day here at the station. Sometimes I pump gas, sometimes I greet customers, sometimes I do paperwork. And sometimes I scrub the toilets which makes me want to repeat the phrase shit, shit, shit over and over to everyone in my pathetic sphere but I don't because my mother says just keep your trap shut, do your job and be the better person.

Now I'm in the inside office and it's paperwork. To be totally specific, I'm doing the statements. Doing the statements is our system of billing the people who don't need to pay for gas or service every time they come in, they can pay one bill at the end of each month. What it means is this: I take all the charge slips we write up for private accounts, add up the amounts, make one bill with a total, staple it to the top and either mail the pack out or drive around and hand deliver them to people. When we hand deliver my mother drives from place to place and I get in and out of the car. She says she hates all that in and out business.

She used to say the same thing when I was younger and played kickball outside with Mary and her brothers. After the third time in, for a root beer or to pee or to grab a crunchy *tarelle* (one of my favorite snacks in the whole world) my mother would look up from whatever she was cooking and say, "In or out. I'm going berserk listening to that door open and close!"

But these days when the in and out is for delivering the statements she says, "It's good for you to get to know people around town. You never know."

"Never know what?" I once asked which she obviously thought was unnecessary. My mother doesn't appreciate when I say unnecessary things and that's why most of the time I get told to not be so fresh. Not to be a smart aleck.

Like everybody else around here my mother thinks it's not what you know, it's who you know. I still cannot figure out how handing a bill to somebody like Ronny Lupetto from Lupetto and Sons or Phil Jurrick from J & R Landscaping could be my saving grace, my hot ticket to a successful future. I'm out of this town as soon as I graduate. Besides, I think what you know counts for something, too. But I try to keep that philosophy to myself because the minute I start talking about knowing things or trying to know things, everybody around here gets nervous.

And that brings me back to the statements. And Sally.

About six months ago, maybe it was last March, I was in the inside office on yet another dreary, depressing Saturday morning. It was the end of the month so I was doing the statements. I came across six slips with nothing but the word Sally written on the line next to Account Name. One was for a tire rotation and the rest for full tanks of gas. I didn't know of any company with the name Sally. I had pumped gas about five times in March (four Saturday mornings and one Thursday night when Chris Monte called in sick) and was never told about any new accounts. So, I asked around.

And this I what I mean about knowing things and making people nervous.

When I asked the guys who pump gas nobody knew anything. When I asked the guys in the shop they ignored me. When I asked Jack he said, "Don't get me started." I went back to the slips and tried to figure out whose handwriting it was. No luck and, of course, nobody initialed the slips like they're supposed to do. So, finally, I asked my father.

"Is there some kind of new company or something with Sally in the name?"

"What? What are you talking about?" He pulled the pack of cigarettes from his front pocket, lit one and tossed the pack onto the desk. He sucked in hard and long and the smoke swirled up toward his eyes. He squinted. He said nothing else.

Then he glared.

"I'm doing the statements and I've got a whole stack here with Sally written on the top but nothing else. No license number, no initials, no last name. I just didn't know."

At this point my heart started beating faster and the inside office suddenly felt like it was shrinking and we were getting closed into the middle together. His glare, that smoky look and all that silence was scaring me. Keep your trap shut. What do you care? The less you know the better. Just get the fucking statements done and don't ask so many questions. Two more years and I'm out of here.

"Just total them and leave the stack on the desk," he said. Then he took another long drag of his cigarette, flicked his ash into his mug of leftover, cold morning coffee and walked out the door toward the pumps.

THE MEN'S ROOM AT FRED'S TEXACO

I am scraping shit off of the inside of the toilet seat in the men's bathroom when Jimmy walks in on me.

"Whoa," he stops short like people do when they try to avoid crashing in a traffic jam. But there's no traffic here. No car traffic or people traffic. It's just Jimmy and me. His work boots screech on the damp gray floor.

"Sorry, Kathy! I, um, I didn't know you were in here."

It looks like he's going to lose his balance. It looks like his long and tall but still strong and sturdy body will tip over and fall right onto me. I am on my knees which makes it easy for me to see his hand quickly pull away from the zipper of his work pants. I've been working at the station long enough now to know that guys do that sometimes. They unzip before they actually get to where they're going.

"No big deal," I say. "Done in a minute."

We lock eyes for one half of a second which causes me to tilt my head to the side and pretend to crack my neck. I do that when I get nervous. And nervous is a monstrosity of an understatement right now.

I spray one more squirt of 409 on the seat, rip a piece of dry paper towel off the roll, and wipe the rim down quickly. Jimmy turns around and mumbles something about coming back in a few minutes. He walks out the door and kicks a bottle cap off the curb and into the parking lot. It was one of a bunch of Heineken caps I swept out from under the bathroom sink just a few minutes before. When I saw all those caps I couldn't help but think: What losers party in the men's john of a Texaco station? Then I remembered how much a six pack of Heineken costs and decided the caps were probably thrown there last night by some fraternity guys from North Jersey who had come down to the Shore for the weekend to get drunk and get laid.

Jimmy's still out there, maybe just to the left or right of the bathroom door and I hear him yell out to Grady, another one of my father's mechanics, who passes by as he whips out of the lot in a blue Trans Am probably testing out the brakes or something. "Hey, Grady, I want my Zeppelin tape back you, asshole!"

"Hey, you," I say, tilting my head out the door, turning toward him. "Why don't you use the Ladies Room? I cleaned that one first. It's all done. Clean and shiny as ever!"

Jimmy appears in the doorway again, this time with a smile that affects the feeling in my kneecaps. For some reason, his boots now whisper, they don't screech.

"Because somebody's in there, too, that's why I'm not using it. Besides it's the Ladies Room. Do I look like a lady to you?"

I crack my neck again.

He reaches his arms up high so his hands touch the top of the rusty metal molding that frames the door. His grey uniform shirt, the one with Jimmy embroidered in red on the side pocket, loosens from under the waist of his pants when he stretches. It rises up just enough to show his belly button and the stream of fine brown hair that runs down from it. I'm still on my knees and in perfect line with his belly. Even though I'm at least three feet away from his body but I swear I think I feel that soft fuzzy stream brush past my lips.

When I stand I am woozy but the elastic on my underwear rides up and feels sticky on my skin so I wiggle my hips to loosen it. First, I'm lucky enough for him to bump into me, literally, while I am scrubby shitty toilets and now I look like a go-go dancer.

Jimmy is still standing there, belly button and all.

I flip the clean seat down hard back on to the bowl and bend over to look down at my knees. Pieces of sand, dirt and black dust stick to my knees. Red marks, from the grout lines in the tile floor, run up and down the front of my legs. I brush them clean with my fingers and even though I'm hunched over I can still see him reach his arm behind his back. From his back pocket, he pulls a crumpled cloth work rag.

The guys in the shop use these rags all day long for a million things. Wiper blades get cleaned with them, hood ornaments get shined up and hands all clean from scrubbing hard with GoJo get dried at the end of each workday. Another one of the glamorous weekly duties of my summer job here at Fred's Texaco is to bag up all the dirty rags and greasy work uniforms and give them to the truck driver who comes to pick up the dirty ones and drop off the clean. My father is known in town as the hard ass who still made all his employees wear uniforms.

"Ain't no way my guys are wearing jeans to work. This is a place of business for God's sake!" I heard him say to my mother one night after work. My brother, still one of the main mechanics in the shop, had decided to tell my father about how some of the guys wanted to wear their own pants to work. How some of them were more comfortable working in Levi's instead of Dickies. That night while I ate my clams and spaghetti and my father and brother argued about the pants I wondered if Jimmy was one of the Dickie-haters. Then I remembered the time I was bagging the uniforms and a pack of rolling papers fell out of the front pocket of Jimmy's pants. The next day was the first time we said more than hi to each other. The day I gave him back his E-Z Widers.

Jimmy is still standing there, smiling and holding the rag. He lifts it up and to the side of where we are standing shakes it out with one flick of his wrist. I imagine dried up fragments of car wax, hand soap and brake grease splashing into the air around us. The very heavy air around us. Blood rushes to my head and soaks into my cheeks.

"Bathroom's a busy place this morning," I say.

The wind swings the door halfway shut so he reaches outside and pulls it closed all the way. More blood rushing. After weeks and weeks of stealing glances and taking the long way back from the soda machine I'm finally alone with this guy. This very cute, tall, strong guy. All I wanted was to brush up against his back while he changed a tire or replaced somebody's headlight. I'm finally alone with him.

And I probably have shit lodged under my fingernails.

He takes another step closer to me and kneels down onto the floor. And this is what happens next: He takes the work rag, folds it in half and rubs it over one of my dirty knees, and then the other. Basically, he's dusting sand from my knees and how that is a turn-on confuses me, but it is. My body shakes from the inside and when I look down the waves in his shaggy brown hair make me dizzy. I don't know if the skin on his hands is warm or cold because it never touches mine, not even one fingertip. Sweating now on the back of my neck and between the shaggy, zig-zag waves and the door being closed shut-tight, tight, tight—and the swirls of 409 around me, I'm loose and woozy. He rubs up and down, back and forth. Slow. Never once does it feel too fast. Or hard. Or wrong. Over my knees, my calves, even my ankles.

And then he stands up straight and tall, strong and sturdy. He folds the dirty rag into a perfect little triangle and slips it down deep into the back pocket of his Dickies.

RESIDUE

It's the boardwalk I tasted first. Lingered there on his tongue.
 The sticky caramel corn and tangy Budweiser. Salt from the ocean.
And on his lips, sweat.
 Warm, too. Everything, warm. The Bud, the night air.
 Me.
 But now, the licorice.

*

Earlier in the night, Berkeley Sweet Shop candy girl asked him, "Red
or black?"
 "One lace," Jimmy said to her. "Black."

*

Now, our tongues. Still searching and tasting, trying to find their way
home. Hard, slow, fast, easy. But gritty, black remains of the licorice rub
against my cheeks. And linger.
 Haunting. Smearing.
 Be a good girl. Be a good girl.

*

When company comes over my mother wears a special apron and usually
makes macaroni with meatballs and a thick meat gravy. Then, after
dinner, she serves Sambuca. Maybe fruit, *finuke* and nuts, too. (Depends
on the company.) And always a small, clear jar filled with black licorice.
There are moments when it all looks very civilized. My father offers the
company cigarettes. I check all the ashtrays and empty them when they
fill up with stubs. Like I'm supposed to do.

*

Jimmy with his wavy brown hair and Adam's apple and Led Zeppelin tee shirt kisses me again and again. But I am gone from here. Miles away from the boardwalk.

All I can taste now is the dreary kitchen at 847 Regency Court, my mother's white apron with the gravy stains and the thick smoke from my father's cigarette.

WAITING FOR THE SONG TO END

Everyone knows that burnouts wear flannel shirts, work boots and faded Levis. And the Levis have rips at the knees. They smoke cigarettes behind the cafeteria doors and in the school bathrooms and when they cut class they sit in their cars behind the 7-Eleven on Coolidge Avenue and use Tampax wrappers to roll joints. They say, "fuck it" and "who gives a fucking shit" about everything. School. Parents. Work. All of it. Safe to say they act like they don't give a fucking shit about anything and so fuck it all. The girls put roach clips on their macramé pocketbook straps and the boys keep Visine in the front pockets of their shirts.

I'm not a burnout.

And that's why now there's sweat and nothing but dizziness. Maybe it's why I'm freaked out, the most freaked out that I've been in a long time, sitting here in the front seat of Jimmy's Trans Am listening to Queen and taking my first hit from a joint he got from Tommy Moreno. Tommy pumps gas on the weekends for my father and always has weed on him.

"He's trouble, that Tommy," my mother never forgets to remind me but then usually confuses things by adding, "but that family, mother of God, they've had their share."

I watch Jimmy inhale. He's the good kind of bad. His eyes take me away from here. Far away. I'm ready to go.

He inhales again and blows the sweet smokiness my way. Then it makes its way through the car. Sweat settles into my creases and hollow spaces. The dizziness is still there but I'm starting to understand it. To like it, even. I gaze at him more. Again. His shirt smells like gasoline and his lips taste like weed and Juicy Fruit. If I could see his voice right now, when he says, "Want another hit, Babe?" it would be a thick navy blue line that leads to a place I've never been to but want to go to. Wonderful and terrifying.

This, all this, is what, just a few years ago when my brother was using all the time, hard and fast, my mother might have called up my brother's alley. Getting high. Running away. I never do this stuff. That was Jack's job. He crashed the tow truck on the way to road calls, stole ten-dollar bills from the jar in my mother's nightgown drawer and took long, angry drags from his cigarettes.

He shot up.

He popped pills.

He smoked weed before every holiday dinner.

Me? I'm Senior Class President, I sit for Mrs. Singer's old aunt who can't be alone at night and I write Statements of Intent and Application Essays for things like the Italian American Club of Ocean County Outstanding Student Scholar Award.

The hit makes me dizzy and the second time Jimmy leans over closer to me he whispers in my ear, "You ready to go in?" His lips are not warm anymore, they're hot. Why is he whispering? The party is a whole front yard away from his car and we are the only ones in it. Maybe when he gets high he whispers or maybe he isn't whispering at all, maybe I'm just thinking he is because that's what happens when you get high. Either way, his lips that are hot, not warm, and the whispering, real or not, just makes me dizzier. But I like it, this dizziness. And that matters, too, because I never liked being dizzy before tonight.

Queen fades out. Springsteen, in.

"Kath, wait," Jimmy says. He slips his hand under my ponytail and loosens it. That's another thing. The burnout ponytail is always loose, never tight. And never is there a ribbon. Only a beige elastic band, like the kind you put around a stack of mail.

"What?"

Now I'm whispering.

"This tune is killer. Let's wait for this song to end before we go in." He turns up the radio and takes one last hit.

Promise me baby you won't let them find us
Hold me in your arms, let's let our love blind us
Cover me, shut the door and cover me
Well I'm looking for a lover who will come on in and cover me.

I know I shouldn't want.

This. Him. All of it. He's older. He's out of school. He fixes cars. He's got a tattoo.

I think I'm supposed to want the opposite of this.

But when he says, "Let's wait for this song to end," I get the wind knocked out of me but it doesn't feel like a ton of bricks or a slap in the face. It feels like water. Warm, clear salty water. He touches my face and my hair and my neck and makes everything loose and long, like my new ponytail and the song.

But then the dizziness disappears and I get the wind knocked out of me again. My father's question slips into me first, sneaky and quiet but then smacks me, hard and fast: Who do you think you are?

I never wait for songs to end. I always want to wait, to listen until the end, to loosen my ponytails. But I never do.

CLOSING TIME

It's the summer after graduation. Until my father finds somebody to replace Chip, the guy who got busted for stealing from the cash box, I'm working at the car wash every day except Sunday. My parents opened the car wash a few months ago on a small piece of property behind what used to be Fred's Texaco but what's now Holiday Service Center. So now the family business is called Holiday Service Center and Car Wash. Which is hilarious and pathetic at the same time.

Holiday is the opposite of what I'm on when I come here. But still, when I answer the phone I get to say: "Holiday, can I help you?"

I get in at 8:00 in the morning and leave at 5:30. I let the last car go through at 5:00 because by the time I count my cash box and record the day's numbers, it's about 5:15 which leaves me the last fifteen minutes to open the safe, put the money in, double check the master water valve and triple check the breakers before locking up.

But yesterday a lady pulled up in an old, rattling Buick at 5:10. I was counting the singles when I looked up and she rolled down her window.

"Sorry, we're closed," I yelled through the opening between the glass door and little office space that is my grotto when we're slow and nobody wants shiny cars. It's where I read and wonder what heaven looks like.

She yelled back.

"Please, Sugar, my girl needs a cleaning real bad."

I shoved the stack of singles in my pocket and walked toward her and her Buick. The hood was speckled with residue of rust and bird shit. Her stubby, dry fingers flew across the dusty, maroon dashboard. Coffee-stained letters and what looked to be unopened bills fell to the floor of the passenger's side.

I leaned into her open window to say, "I started closing out my cash box already, ma'am-sorry" but then I smelled a weird combination of salami and rubbing alcohol. My eyes moved from her fingers to her hair which was black and greasy, but some was gone. Portions of her scalp showed.

"Yeah, I guess she kinda does," I said, and turned away to look at the main operating panel that held the buttons for all the washes and waxes and shine options.

Then I looked at the grimy hood of her Buick, the car she calls *her girl.*

Then I looked at the hairless spots on her head.

"Please, Sugar," she pleaded, "I got a five here somewhere." She turned away and opened the glove compartment. Now it was ketchup packets and what looked like an old black and white photograph of a man in a soldier's uniform that fell to the floor, landing on top of the letters and bills.

"Why don't you go ahead and take your foot off the brake and put it in neutral, ma'am. I got this one today."

Free washes don't happen every day here. My father says it's company policy to save the free washes for good customers, people who are regulars. Don't even get me started with that.

But I never saw this woman before. Not even once. Definitely not a regular.

She's very much irregular.

And that's the reality that knocked me down. Her irregularity and all that went with it—the smell of salami, the bird shit, the old ketchup packets, her girl: the Buick—all of this, all of a sudden, mattered.

I thought, *What if?*

I imagined her sitting in a fancy, swiveling beauty parlor chair, her legs crossed, a cup of tea in one hand and a slick magazine in the other, her hair being styled in a shiny high beehive.

I looked one more time at the soldier boy on the floor.

Then I pushed hard on the blue button labeled "The Works at Holiday" and watched her and her girl fade into the last wash of the day.

WAITING BY WINDOWS III

Jimmy said he'd park down by the Wilsons. I told him to be here by 11:30 because when my father is home and not in Atlantic City, my parents fall asleep in bed watching the eleven o'clock news. It's 11:20. I checked them ten minutes ago. He was snoring and she was out cold. Thank you, God.

I pull the curtains to the side and peer out my bedroom window. I can't believe myself. I can't believe me. And we're not even going to do it tonight. He knows that. I'm still not ready so it's not even about doing it. It's not about that at all. He says he'll wait forever if that's what it takes. I realize how dumb and corny and silly that sounds but do I care?

No.

Today when I got home from school I put some Vaseline on the tracks of the screen and carried two cinder blocks from the backyard into the front. I put them next to the outside of the house right under my bedroom window. The last thing I want is for the screen to screech when I open it or for Jimmy to break an arm trying to scale the bricks on our house.

But it's not 11:30 yet, it's 11:20, so I'm still waiting by my window hoping he gets here soon. And when he does, I'll let him in.

DESIRE

No one can find my brother anywhere and my father is making a mess. "I got three lifts tied up cause of this shit!" he hurls.

Lifts. Why did he have to mention the lifts?

Two nights ago, Jimmy was at the shop working late on some old lady's Cutlass and I was there, too, reading and keeping him company.

"Hey babe, do me a favor," he said. When I'm home from college on breaks and he calls me babe everything kind of stands still. So I said sure.

"Check the backseat. See if my adjustable is back there." I climbed into the back and the whole car moved up. Into the air. Off of the ground. He activated the lift, hopped up into the driver's seat and then flipped his body over, into the back. He laughed and we kissed and I realized there was no missing wrench. It was only us, the rising Cutlass and desire. The kind of desire that can change everything.

* * *

Father screams again. "This is a business for God's sake! I'm trying to run a fucking business here and this is the thanks I get."

My father's brown eyes are smaller and a shade lighter than mine. And they're cold. They pinch so I look away. Then his cigarette ashes fall onto the pile of work orders and bills I am supposed to be filing. Filing. Part of my job, too. Instead I'm now being told to get my ass in gear and head to Jersey Stan's Tanks and Welding to get the torch tank filled. This tank is real important around here, it keeps the blowtorches up and running. Blowtorches are what the guys use to melt rusty nuts and bolts and cut up old exhaust systems.

"C'mon," my father says to me, "pull your car around and I'll have Grady put the empty tank in your trunk. And where the hell is your brother?"

No one can find my brother and my father is making a mess.

My father and I are standing next to the desk in what we all call the inside office at the station. It's the office in the back where only family, certain employees, and a few of his *paisans* are allowed. It's a lot different than the front office, the waiting room. Fresh film of Pine-Sol on the floor, fresh pot of coffee on the counter and fresh batch of Italian cookies in a can next to the rows of Styrofoam coffee cups. Stacks of *Women's Day*, *Reader's Digest* and *The National Enquirer* sit in piles on the end table reminding the crowd of others who are missing and messed up.

Pictures of my family line the painted concrete walls. We had to use masonry nails to hang them. There's one of my brother at age five sitting on the curb in front of the door to Fred's Texaco. There's one of my mother, pencil lodged behind her ear, blowing kisses to the camera and standing at the service counter greeting customers. Then there's one of all of us, all the Pontorieros, sitting around the dinner table on Christmas Eve eating shrimp and scallops and smelts.

The inside office is a different story. Most of the paperwork on the desk is stained with one thing or another: cigarette ashes, pizza sauce, coffee.

And if you look a little closer: blood, sweat and tears.

FILLING THE TORCH TANK

The shirt says Welders Do It with A Hot Rod. I try to keep my eyes on his hair and his face. But then I wonder: How does someone with such blond curls and smooth little boy skin wear a shirt this raunchy?

He scribbles a receipt for the air tank, the one I brought here to Jersey Stan's twenty minutes ago to get filled, and the one I need to get back to the shop.

Little boy skin answers the phone and looks out the window. I peek at his shirt again. Welders Do It with A Hot Rod. It's gray with green letters and has a picture of some dude with a welder's mask on holding a blowtorch in one hand and a beer in the other. It's beyond ridiculous.

He swings around and catches me. "Like my shirt?"

"Can you just put the tank in my trunk so I can get out of here?" I want to call him a dick but it doesn't happen.

"You bet I can, sugar."

He smirks. He chuckles. He winks, even. He takes a pack of Wrigley's Spearmint from his front pocket, unwraps a piece, folds it onto his tongue and pushes the pack toward me. "Want some?"

And then, I burn.

Inside. Outside. Up. And down. As far down as I go, as far as I am, I burn.

I yank the receipt from the counter and head toward the door. His eyes are on my ass. I actually feel them there. The knob on the door and it is hot and slimy. Something sticky that belongs in a car, on a pipe, or in a tube rubs off onto my fingers.

I hate this fucking job. I want to be back at school talking about Raymond Carver, Piaget's Stages of Development and the Kung Bushmen of the Kalahari.

And no one can find my brother. And my father is making a mess.

He bends over and lifts the heavy cylinder-shaped tank off the ground and into his arms. He cradles it and shuffles a few steps from the filling station on the side of the garage to my old, black Monte Carlo. His work pants are a little long and the bottom of each leg is worn and fringed. A tattoo of an eagle blazes the inside of his left forearm. I open the trunk, brush my books to the side and step back. He places the heavy tank inside and puts my books on either side of it so it won't roll around. He's careful, gentle even.

Every time I go to pick up or deliver tanks my father warns me how these tanks can "blow the hell up" if they get hit. "Watch yourself on the road coming back with those tanks, Kathy. Don't take no chances out there."

"Take it slow, now, little lady," raunchy tee shirt guy warns me. He checks the cap on the tank very carefully and slides his hand over the thick cold metal before shutting my trunk.

I plunge into the driver's seat. Having trouble exhaling again. I remember the tank and his hand and wonder what it looks like when he touches his girlfriend. Why am I thinking this? I burn again. Little lady? Fuck him! My Monte Carlo leather burns through my jeans and onto the backs of my thighs. I turn on the ignition and imagine what she looks like—the girlfriend—and fan myself with the take-out menu from Mickey's Deli. Pat Benatar's on the radio reminding me about how much of a battlefield love is.

She probably wears Red Candies. Red Candies with tight jeans and black tube tops. The jeans are probably so tight that when he slides them off, crimson valleys linger around her belly button and down the sides of her legs.

I turn up the radio, do a U-ie right in the middle of the dirt parking lot of Jersey Stan's and careen onto Route 9 heading south back toward Holiday.

III. ONE MORE THING ABOUT NOW

"Stay together," my mother said to us, over and over and over again. Now, as my sisters, Lucy and Maria, my brother, Jack, and I tackle and take on life, motherless and fatherless, with children and grandchildren of our own, I'm so glad she never stopped repeating that phrase.

Over and over again, "Stay together."

I know they have their own truths, their own understandings of these memories, these years, these dramas. I honor that. So, as with most stories, this is not the whole story. It's just part of it. My part.

Which brings me to the handful of hallelujahs uttered on the day, deep into the writing of this collection, I realized there was no way in hell I could write the whole story, even if I tried.

And, come to think of it, I did try. That's what got me into trouble. That's a little of what made me want to run and hide when kind, curious souls asked, "So what's your manuscript about anyway?"

What's the story?

Again, I wanted to answer. Nothing came out.

So, I did what came natural when I was a young girl, in the years illustrated in this book. I eavesdropped, but this time mostly on myself: past, present and future. I wondered, but this time mostly about the ferocity of both love and forgiveness. I was still on the receiving end of rhetorical questions but, with both of my parents deceased, I was the one left asking.

Happy now?

Satisfied?

Are you finished?

Who do you think you are?

I traipsed into the memories again and paid very close attention to what I thought mattered, what stuck to the walls of my girlwoman consciousness of today. I dug deeper, lingering on the tiny, ordinary recollections of my family, home, culture and identity; what Sandra Cisneros calls the "jar of buttons."

Some answers never materialized but, in time, some surfaced. Never did I think they would appear, as they did, in things like hairdos, boyfriends, pots of macaroni, sock and underwear drawers and dirty fingernails. And never did I imagine the strange potion of reconciliation, comfort and acceptance that can rise and purify when offered time and space to remember, without judgement.

Magic.

Which particular snapshots I reimagined on these pages was not a deliberate decision. The memories were and still are haphazard and curious to me. In many ways, the collection was always there—my very own jar of buttons. What was deliberate was this, though: the tossing of these memories without analysis and psychobabble. I unscrewed the cap and spilled the buttons. But this time, instead of trying to clean up the spill, the mess, the *everything*, I honored where they landed and worked from there.

And there took me to here.

Home.

BIG THANKS

In addition to darkness, one of my greatest fears is forgetting to thank those who deserve thanks. So, you can see why the crafting of this page is enough to make me want to run for the hills, dig a deep hole and hide. But then, I'd have to deal with darkness.

So here goes. Big thanks to:

- the state of NJ, for getting under my skin and staying there
- the state of NY, for letting me cross the border in 1986 (and not having any sort of rule pertaining to the number of times, in one's life, that crossing can occur)
- all the musicians whose tunes on the radio, and on 8-tracks, cassettes, CDs and, more recently, Spotify playlists, pushed and pulled me up and down the Garden State Parkway and the New Jersey Turnpike during the years depicted in this book
- my academic, creative and professional illuminators, Olivia Croom, Nic Grosso, Dr. Anthony Tamburri, Dr. Fred Gardaphé, Kathryn Gurfein, Jane Brox, Pat Dunn, Maria Guira, Olivia Kate Cerrone, Tony Ardizzone, Jo Ann Beard, Vijay Seshadri, Suzanne Gardinier, Nick Flynn, Alice Truax, Chuck Wachtel, Carolyn McLaughlin, Ann Imig , Kelly Caldwell, Julie Evans, Mihai Grunfeld, Ed McCann, Bill Papaleo, Cooper Lee Bombardier, Meg Walker, Gretchen Koss, Jeanne-Marie Fleming, Joelle Sander and her Art of Memoir students, my colleagues at Montclair State University, 650 Where Writers Read, The Writing Institute at Sarah Lawrence College, The Joe Papaleo Writers' Workshop in Cetara, Italy, the 2012 NYC cast of Listen to Your Mother, Italian American Writers Association, Bread Loaf Writers in Sicily, the Fairfield University's Summer Writers Conference and, finally, the memories of Jean Marzollo, Lina Brock, Joe Papaleo, Esther Broner and Regina Arnold, for shining your lights along my way

- my writing mentors, Steven Lewis and Irene O'Garden, for your generosity, wisdom and time
- Bordighera Press, for supporting my work and finding a place for my stories
- my students, each and every one of them, for teaching me
- my wholehearted and hearty circle of family, friends and comrades for beautiful, stormy drama, tight bonds and endless cups of coffee
- the squad who knows me longer than anyone else on this planet, Lucy, Ria and Jack, for acceptance, compassion and text messages that no one else but us can understand
- my parents, Catherine and Fred Pontoriero, for the tenacious love
- AJ, Maya, Maisy and Sam, for the faith you instill and the magic you make, each and every day
- and to Peppe, for being the love of my life.

A final note: Some of the chapters in this collection were previously published, at times in different formats, in the following publications: *Ovunque Siamo, Lumina, Junk-A Literary Fix, The Mom Egg* and *VIA: Voices in Italian Americana*. I am grateful to the editorial teams for including my stories in their volumes.

ABOUT THE AUTHOR

KATHY CURTO teaches at Montclair State University and The Writing Institute at Sarah Lawrence College. Her work has been published in the essay collection, *Listen to Your Mother: What She Said Then, What We're Saying Now*, and in *The New York Times, Barrelhouse, La Voce di New York, Drift, Talking Writing, Junk, The Inquisitive Eater, The Asbury Park Press, VIA: Voices in Italian Americana, Ovunque Siamo* and *Lumina*. She has been the recipient of the Kathryn Gurfein Writing Fellowship, the Montclair State University Engaged Teaching Fellowship and also serves on the faculty of the Joe Papaleo Writers' Workshop in Cetara, Italy. Kathy lives in the Hudson Valley with her husband and their four children. This is her first book.

CONSTANCE SANCETTA. *Here in Cerchio*. Vol 93. Local History. $15

MARIA MAZZIOTTI GILLAN. *Ancestors' Song*. Vol 92. Poetry. $14

MICHAEL PARENTI. *Waiting for Yesterday: Pages from a Street Kid's Life*. Vol 90. Memoir. $15

ANNIE LANZILLOTTO. *Schistsong*. Vol 89. Poetry. $15

EMANUEL DI PASQUALE. *Love Lines*. Vol 88. Poetry. $10

CAROSONE & LOGIUDICE. *Our Naked Lives*. Vol 87. Essays. $15

JAMES PERICONI. *Strangers in a Strange Land: A Survey of Italian-Language American Books*.Vol 86. Book History. $24

DANIELA GIOSEFFI. *Escaping La Vita Della Cucina*. Vol 85. Essays. $22

MARIA FAMÀ. *Mystics in the Family*. Vol 84. Poetry. $10

ROSSANA DEL ZIO. *From Bread and Tomatoes to Zuppa di Pesce "Ciambotto"*. Vol. 83. $15

LORENZO DELBOCA. *Polentoni*. Vol 82. Italian Studies. $15

SAMUEL GHELLI. *A Reference Grammar*. Vol 81. Italian Language. $36

ROSS TALARICO. *Sled Run*. Vol 80. Fiction. $15

FRED MISURELLA. *Only Sons*. Vol 79. Fiction. $14

FRANK LENTRICCHIA. *The Portable Lentricchia*. Vol 78. Fiction. $16

RICHARD VETERE. *The Other Colors in a Snow Storm*. Vol 77. Poetry. $10

GARIBALDI LAPOLLA. *Fire in the Flesh*. Vol 76 Fiction & Criticism. $25

GEORGE GUIDA. *The Pope Stories*. Vol 75 Prose. $15

ROBERT VISCUSI. *Ellis Island*. Vol 74. Poetry. $28

ELENA GIANINI BELOTTI. *The Bitter Taste of Strangers Bread*. Vol 73. Fiction. $24

PINO APRILE. *Terroni*. Vol 72. Italian Studies. $20

EMANUEL DI PASQUALE. *Harvest*. Vol 71. Poetry. $10

ROBERT ZWEIG. *Return to Naples*. Vol 70. Memoir. $16

AIROS & CAPPELLI. *Guido*. Vol 69. Italian/American Studies. $12

FRED GARDAPHÉ. *Moustache Pete is Dead! Long Live Moustache Pete!*. Vol 67. Literature/Oral History. $12

PAOLO RUFFILLI. *Dark Room/Camera oscura*. Vol 66. Poetry. $11

HELEN BAROLINI. *Crossing the Alps*. Vol 65. Fiction. $14

COSMO FERRARA. *Profiles of Italian Americans*. Vol 64. Italian Americana. $16

GIL FAGIANI. *Chianti in Connecticut*. Vol 63. Poetry. $10

BASSETTI & D'ACQUINO. *Italic Lessons*. Vol 62. Italian/American Studies. $10

CAVALIERI & PASCARELLI, Eds. *The Poet's Cookbook*. Vol 61. Poetry/Recipes. $12

EMANUEL DI PASQUALE. *Siciliana*. Vol 60. Poetry. $8

NATALIA COSTA, Ed. *Bufalini*. Vol 59. Poetry. $18.

RICHARD VETERE. *Baroque*. Vol 58. Fiction. $18.

LEWIS TURCO. *La Famiglia/The Family*. Vol 57. Memoir. $15

NICK JAMES MILETI. *The Unscrupulous*. Vol 56. Humanities. $20

BASSETTI. ACCOLLA. D'AQUINO. *Italici: An Encounter with Piero Bassetti*. Vol 55. Italian Studies. $8

GIOSE RIMANELLI. *The Three-legged One*. Vol 54. Fiction. $15

CHARLES KLOPP. *Bele Antiche Stòrie*. Vol 53. Criticism. $25

JOSEPH RICAPITO. *Second Wave*. Vol 52. Poetry. $12

GARY MORMINO. *Italians in Florida*. Vol 51. History. $15

GIANFRANCO ANGELUCCI. *Federico F.* Vol 50. Fiction. $15

ANTHONY VALERIO. *The Little Sailor*. Vol 49. Memoir. $9

ROSS TALARICO. *The Reptilian Interludes*. Vol 48. Poetry. $15

RACHEL GUIDO DE VRIES. *Teeny Tiny Tino's Fishing Story*. Vol 47. Children's Literature. $6

EMANUEL DI PASQUALE. *Writing Anew*. Vol 46. Poetry. $15

MARIA FAMÀ. *Looking For Cover*. Vol 45. Poetry. $12

ANTHONY VALERIO. *Toni Cade Bambara's One Sicilian Night*. Vol 44. Poetry. $10

EMANUEL CARNEVALI. *Furnished Rooms*. Vol 43. Poetry. $14

BRENT ADKINS. et al., Ed. *Shifting Borders. Negotiating Places*. Vol 42. Conference. $18

GEORGE GUIDA. *Low Italian*. Vol 41. Poetry. $11

GARDAPHÈ, GIORDANO, TAMBURRI. *Introducing Italian Americana*. Vol 40. Italian/American Studies. $10

DANIELA GIOSEFFI. *Blood Autumn/Autunno di sangue*. Vol 39. Poetry. $15/$25

FRED MISURELLA. *Lies to Live By*. Vol 38. Stories. $15

STEVEN BELLUSCIO. *Constructing a Bibliography*. Vol 37. Italian Americana. $15

ANTHONY JULIAN TAMBURRI, Ed. *Italian Cultural Studies 2002*. Vol 36. Essays. $18

BEA TUSIANI. *con amore*. Vol 35. Memoir. $19

FLAVIA BRIZIO-SKOV, Ed. *Reconstructing Societies in the Aftermath of War*. Vol 34. History. $30

TAMBURRI. et al., Eds. *Italian Cultural Studies 2001*. Vol 33. Essays. $18

ELIZABETH G. MESSINA, Ed. *In Our Own Voices*. Vol 32. Italian/American Studies. $25

STANISLAO G. PUGLIESE. *Desperate Inscriptions*. Vol 31. History. $12

HOSTERT & TAMBURRI, Eds. *Screening Ethnicity*. Vol 30. Italian/American Culture. $25

G. PARATI & B. LAWTON, Eds. *Italian Cultural Studies*. Vol 29. Essays. $18

HELEN BAROLINI. *More Italian Hours*. Vol 28. Fiction. $16

FRANCO NASI, Ed. *Intorno alla Via Emilia*. Vol 27. Culture. $16

ARTHUR L. CLEMENTS. *The Book of Madness & Love*. Vol 26. Poetry. $10

JOHN CASEY, et al. *Imagining Humanity*. Vol 25. Interdisciplinary Studies. $18

ROBERT LIMA. *Sardinia/Sardegna*. Vol 24. Poetry. $10

DANIELA GIOSEFFI. *Going On*. Vol 23. Poetry. $10

ROSS TALARICO. *The Journey Home*. Vol 22. Poetry. $12

EMANUEL DI PASQUALE. *The Silver Lake Love Poems*. Vol 21. Poetry. $7

JOSEPH TUSIANI. *Ethnicity*. Vol 20. Poetry. $12

JENNIFER LAGIER. *Second Class Citizen*. Vol 19. Poetry. $8

FELIX STEFANILE. *The Country of Absence*. Vol 18. Poetry. $9

PHILIP CANNISTRARO. *Blackshirts*. Vol 17. History. $12

LUIGI RUSTICHELLI, Ed. *Seminario sul racconto*. Vol 16. Narrative. $10

LEWIS TURCO. *Shaking the Family Tree*. Vol 15. Memoirs. $9

LUIGI RUSTICHELLI, Ed. *Seminario sulla drammaturgia*. Vol 14. Theater/ Essays. $10

FRED GARDAPHÈ. *Moustache Pete is Dead! Long Live Moustache Pete!*. Vol 13. Oral Literature. $10

JONE GAILLARD CORSI. *Il libretto d'autore. 1860–1930*. Vol 12. Criticism. $17

HELEN BAROLINI. *Chiaroscuro: Essays of Identity*. Vol 11. Essays. $15

PICARAZZI & FEINSTEIN, Eds. *An African Harlequin in Milan*. Vol 10. Theater/Essays. $15

JOSEPH RICAPITO. *Florentine Streets & Other Poems*. Vol 9. Poetry. $9

FRED MISURELLA. *Short Time*. Vol 8. Novella. $7

NED CONDINI. *Quartettsatz*. Vol 7. Poetry. $7

ANTHONY JULIAN TAMBURRI, Ed. *Fuori: Essays by Italian/American Lesbians and Gays*. Vol 6. Essays. $10

ANTONIO GRAMSCI. P. Verdicchio. Trans. & Intro. *The Southern Question*. Vol 5.Social Criticism. $5

DANIELA GIOSEFFI. *Word Wounds & Water Flowers*. Vol 4. Poetry. $8

WILEY FEINSTEIN. *Humility's Deceit: Calvino Reading Ariosto Reading Calvino*. Vol 3. Criticism. $10

PAOLO A. GIORDANO, Ed. *Joseph Tusiani: Poet. Translator. Humanist*. Vol 2. Criticism. $25

ROBERT VISCUSI. *Oration Upon the Most Recent Death of Christopher Columbus*. Vol 1. Poetry.

BIO CURTO

Curto, Kathy
Not for nothing :
 glimpses into a Jersey

02/28/19

CPSIA information can be obtained
at www.ICGtesting.com
Printed in the USA
FSHW011522191218

9 781599 541297